A TALL TAILOR, TOO

FUNNY THINGS ARE TRUE

CL WARDELL

ISBN-13: 9798579074164

Cover design by: Art Painter
Library of Congress Control Number: 2018675309
Printed in the United States of America

TABLE OF CONTENTS

CL WARDELL

RETIREMENT: MILESTONE OR MILLSTONE?

With retirement looming, well-intentioned contemporaries cautioned me about the risks involved; uniformly they urged me to find something to do after leaving the workplace. The alternative, dire indeed, was death by inactivity within six months. As I cleared my desk and packed my boxes, one of my colleagues took me aside and confessed her envy- she wished that she had *my* money so she, too, could retire. I explained to her my long, disciplined program of preparing and executing a financial game plan to ensure a comfortable post-work life. "It may be true," I told her, "that with the exercise of judicious frugality, I may be able to live comfortably in retirement with the following caveat- I can only afford to live for those six months you tell me that I have left." If my colleagues were correct and my numbers bear out, I've prepared just well enough to bounce my last check to the crematorium. What ensues on these pages then, is not some ego-driven effort to record a particularly compelling story, but the desperate, death-defying do-something enterprise of a dude doomed by demography.

I reflect back on the concatenation of choices that got me to here, to the final curtain on the drama that was a long life of labor, and it dawns on me that one defining moment was my decision to attend computer school. This decision confounds for a couple of reasons; I had zero interest in being a computer programmer, specifically, or pursuing a career in general. It was evident early on that I had not a corporate soul, but a feeling that any job confining me to a cubicle in an office would be soul-crushing. The "wide open spaces" had great appeal, that vast area beyond the end of the toll roads west of Chicago that I discovered while driving coast-to-coast on vacation with my family as a twelve-year-old, and my heart became set on emulating the truckers who slept in beds in their trucks and blew their air horns for children when prompted. Even though my truck-driving lifestyle had provided fulfillment to date, it was a seasonal layoff that led me to the unemployment office where I was identified as a viable candidate for a CETA position. CETA, an acronym for the Comprehensive Education and Training Act, was an early 1980's stimulus program designed to move the unemployed into employment; if qualified, the state would continue to pay benefits plus cover the cost of tuition while the candidate attended school for six months. Despite a head-scratching career move, this seemed an opportunity worth pursuing, so I sat for the entrance exam and enrolled in class. As the course wound down, I conformed to institutional protocol and scheduled my first job interview, an otherworldly experience for me. Dressed in a suit and tie to apply for a "real" job felt strange (as it might today- hoodies and cargo shorts seem more likely attire for this century's programmers) and I became unsettled as the interviewer yammered about how awesome my previous trucking experiences must have been. "You are correct, sir, that I had the opportunity to see the country without a boss looking over my shoulder, but I believe this programming course has prepared me to move forward and begin a new chapter in my life." He appeared mystified that I would forsake such a romantic-seeming lifestyle in order to program computers, causing me to reflect, reconsider and rethink my options; my pretensions about finding a "real" job were over. I phoned a friend in the trucking business and delivered a load to Maspeth, Queens, in New York City the night I received my programming certificate and was back on the road.

As it happened, I never became a computer programmer, but remained engaged in the transportation industry for another forty years, until my retirement in 2019. I transitioned into management, but I never shook my own romantic notions about life on the road, so I found myself back "jamming gears" in 2010, after accepting an early retirement offer from Duke University. To my chagrin, but hardly to my surprise, I discovered that most everything had changed- trucks had evolved, of course; made quieter and more comfortable, with amenities like air-conditioning, air-ride suspensions and much more horsepower. My truck had upper and lower bunks and enough headroom to dress while standing. To accommodate the influx of women who were attracted to driving jobs, truck stops had changed as well- restrooms with separate showers cleaned after every use! Of course, I, too, had changed fairly dramatically, and the curmudgeon that I had become resented the corporate makeover of everything that I had formerly found dear. Charming mom-and-pop truck stops that once competed for business became, like the airlines, three or four bland business entities devoid of personality- trucker buffets replaced by franchised junk-food and microwavable sandwiches. Perhaps this explained why refrigerators and microwaves were now standard features in many new trucks. The "white line fever" I had experienced as a younger man had become a corporate "bottom line fever"- everything standardized to cut costs and maximize returns. Exiting the interstate anywhere in the U.S. and confronting the same scarcity of appealing options, I despaired for the loss of local character and lasted a mere six months before parking the truck one last time.

Now retired for good, with a truckload of memories and plenty of time on my hands (okay, six months, tops), I record these memories as a tribute to that poor deskbound data jockey in Human Resources who interviewed me all those years ago, and others of his ilk who dreamed of doing something wildly different with their lives. The book's subtitle derives, respectfully, from Bill Callahan, a musician who released his initial album in 1990 and described his long-time lyrical inspiration, in a June 10, 2019 interview in *New Yorker* magazine, by saying "Humor opens a door in people. Funny things are true." "Dude," I thought to myself, "you've found your muse." So many funny, true things kept me sane during a lifetime of labor that I decided to record "a tall tale or two" and offer them herein. Let's open some doors.

BABY BOOMERS

"I'd like to die in my sleep like my grandfather. Not screaming in terror like the passengers in the back seat of his car."   Will Rogers

W hen my grandmother flew to North Carolina in 1975 for my brother's wedding, her grandchildren were amazed to learn that it was the first time in her long life that she had been on an airplane. What seemed even more fantastic was that she could recall, as a young child at the beginning of the last century, the Wright brothers first flight. Wow. Here was someone who had experienced the history of aviation from the first flight (twelve seconds, one hundred and twenty feet) to landing humans on the moon (eight days, 953,000 miles); I still find it hard to believe that the entirety of aviation history had unwound in a single lifetime. In the arc of my life, I can recall nothing like it.

There were 76.4 million Baby Boomers at their peak in 1964. Because of that immense number, they came to be defined by the descriptive statistical term "pig in a python," (the population bulge moving along the timeline as they aged) and were notable mostly for their "Youth Culture" impact on marketing and advertising. The magnitude of anything like my grandmother's experience- born on a small farm in New York City at the end of the nineteenth century (before automobiles!) and watching men set foot on the moon (from a rocket ship!) years later, still astounds. Her children's generation survived the Depression and won a world war; Baby Boomers spent a weekend of intermittent rain showers at Woodstock and bragged about toughing it out to the "Star Spangled Banner" finale by Jimi Hendrix. To succeeding generations of Millennials and Generation Xers, the high-tech boom replaced the space race of orbiting satellites by rival superpowers as the background music to their lifetime experience, but shopping from a cellphone with next-day delivery hardly conveys the same awe as walking on the moon. Without a doubt, "Boomers," by their sheer numbers, precipitated structural changes in society, but their grand gestures and burning desires- burning draft cards to protest the war in Southeast Asia, burning bras to protest the second-class status of women and burning cities to highlight the plight of the urban poor and the treatment of minorities- were attempts to focus attention on the mess made by the "Silent Majority". As ground-breaking and (r)evolutionary as these might have been, they now seem quaint. Baby Boomers may have agitated for dramatic change, but culturally, social media overwhelmed social progress as a thing, and a class of tech entrepreneurs, amassing obscene fortunes, managed to mock the very notion of social responsibility. Go figure.

EARLY MEMORIES

I was a wee lad, a first grader, when I recall getting into trouble for my sense of humor for the first time. At that age I had no concept of a sense of humor, of course, I only recognized my ability to make classmates laugh, and, in tandem with that, of focusing the teacher's attention on me. Birth order is one determinant of personality and I was a middle child. Middle children, it has been demonstrated, typically receive less attention at home than first and last siblings, so perhaps I was compensating for that deficiency. Technically, I was one of a pair of middle children, since there were four of us. I had two older female siblings and a younger brother, so I was more of a lower-middle child and my sister- one school grade ahead of me- was the upper-middle child. Our age differentials merely compounded the problem; she went off to school the year my brother was born so I never enjoyed the sole ministrations of my stay-at-home mother. This may explain my stunted Emotional Quotient as well as the delight I took in my teacher's attention, even after she scheduled "a talk" with my parents. When educators mention one's "Permanent Record" they are not kidding about the adjective. Either my record defined me for a generation or I was predisposed to get into trouble, since Miss Murray (ah, yes, Rose Murray, my first-grade teacher and my first crush) was only one of many teachers through my formative years to schedule "a talk" with my parents about my behavior in class. As a student, it was unlikely that I would follow in the footsteps of this sister who was in the class ahead of me; she was extremely conscientious, worked very hard and set the bar way too high. I'm certain that hers was middle-child compensation of a much more productive form. Instead of "look at me, I'm funny!" it was "look at me, I'm smart!" She graduated as class valedictorian and teachers hoping for a clone when I showed up got a clown instead. She was smart, I was a smart-ass. While the payout for academic distinction had to wait until the end of the quarter, or semester or, in my sister's case, her high school career, a good laugh was immediately reinforcing. So, even though I was bright enough, I could not sustain an academic focus. Instead, the quick quip or one-liner would have to suffice. For example: my Latin teacher, a really delightful and dapper older man who had lost an arm during the first world war, put his spit-polished wingtip on the frame of my desk one day and proceeded to tie it with one hand. "I'll bet that you can't do that," he said. My sister doubtless could have rendered the coup de grace in flawless Latin (but wouldn't), so I responded immediately in English- "I bet you can't do it with two hands." Veni, Vedi, Vici. I came, I saw, I got the laugh. I passed Latin but failed English Composition because, again, I went for the gag instead of the grade. Our first assignment was to write a "get to know you" five-hundred-word essay on our greatest personal asset or biggest liability; I turned in a paper titled "My Greatest Asset" comprised of the single word "Brevity." Clever? I thought so. Intellectually lazy? Most likely. I failed this assignment despite a well-reasoned argument that five-hundred words about being brief was oxymoronic. Given an opportunity to submit a second paper to repair the damage and improve my grade, I changed my approach thematically, retitled my essay to "My Biggest Liability," changed "Brevity" to "Levity" and resubmitted my effort. Stubborn? Yes, but it is never prudent to butt heads with the teacher. Surprise! I got the same result and had to retake the course because it was a graduation requirement.

When it came to labor, though, I displayed a fortitude lacking in the classroom. Although I had cut grass and shoveled snow for neighbors, my first real employment was at a car wash. The joint was open from 8:00 in the morning until 8:30 in the evening Monday through Saturday and 8:00 to 5:00 on Sunday. The summer I turned sixteen, if it was open, I was there. Eighty-three hours a week at minimum wage ($1.25 per hour in 1964) -straight pay, no time-and-a-half premium- and yet $103.75 for eighty-three hours was a veritable fortune for this sixteen-year-old. Plus tips! Unless it rained there were no days off, and no benefits with the following exceptions: I learned how to drive thanks to the "on the job training program" (I was self-taught on 4-speed Corvettes and Mustangs, sparing the clutch on the family sedan) and those long work days prepared me for the hours I could expect in the future as a truck driver. Thus began my first affair in a lifelong relationship with transportation. Two years later I joined the union and worked as a Teamster, which was remunerative enough that I stuck with it through trucking deregulation and OPEC (The Organization of the Petroleum Exporting Countries, known colloquially as the "oil cartel" manipulated oil output; during the Carter administration this created fuel shortages that resulted in price inflation, long gas lines and odd/even days of fuel availability), commercial driver testing and licensing (during the Reagan administration), increasing traffic, deteriorating infrastructure and a changing natural and cultural landscape for over twenty years. I got a withdrawal card from the union in 1989, but remain a member in good standing.

Let's go back to school. I survived Miss Murray's class, a few more Parent-Teacher conferences, a move to a new city (involving a job transfer and not on-going discipline issues) and decided to join the band in the fourth grade. I signed up to play the saxophone because I loved the look and the sound of the instrument, and my father, a "big band" fan, listened to the Dorsey brothers. Jimmy Dorsey played the saxophone, and something about that intricate brass instrument caught my fancy. At our first band meeting we handed in our instrumental requests with our permission slips and were dismissed. When we reconvened, the music director discussed his dilemma- although he had a number of sax enthusiasts, his brass section was lacking a trombone player. Taking a look around the room he spotted me standing in the back, about a head taller than most of the other students, and recruited me. First, let me say that I spent my formative years at the back of the room. Teachers routinely sorted by the first initial of our last name or by height; either way I was almost always at the end of the line or in the back of the room. Second, the slide trombone requires long enough arms to play the scale, so my lengthy limbs might have been an advantage. But, heck, Jimmy Dorsey's brother Tommy and the very famous Glenn Miller both played the trombone, so I complied. I played in the band through the ninth grade, when I gave it up for a couple of reasons. Reason #1- parents. My parents had encouraged my participation in band and orchestra and paid for private lessons but, whenever they entertained, I dreaded a call from them to bring the instrument downstairs. If the call came after a couple of martinis, they would ask me to play something. A few more cocktails and my father would take the horn and bleat out some breathy, discordant farting noise to the hilarious delight of his well-oiled guests. Reason #2- high school. The summer before my sophomore year I was invited to join the high school marching band. One practice on an asphalt parking lot in the August heat was all it took for me to explore other options. Addendum to Reason #2- girls. I had difficulty picturing myself wooing girlfriends in a band uniform. I had become incredibly self-conscious (probably because I had also become a teenager) and a band uniform simply presented one more obstacle to overcome, particularly since the uniform in question was nowhere near long enough to accommodate my very long legs, which started at my ankles, as legs typically do, but ended somewhere near my chest. My young grandson has rendered some remarkably accurate drawings of my former self- stick figures of a head with legs and arms. He didn't even know me then! Instead, I decided to devote my extracurricular activities to more manly pursuits, like the Ski Club. I didn't ski but I knew someone who did, and she was inspiration enough to pursue membership in the Ski Club. Being in this club would allow me to spend long hours with her on the bus trips to the mountains of northern New England, where, on our first outing I assured her that, yes, of course I could ski. (How difficult could it be? It's just gravity, for crying out loud). I discovered on my first attempt that it was far more difficult than real skiers made it look. The closest I had ever come to skiing was a summertime visit, years earlier, to Squaw Valley, in California, the site of the 1960 Winter Olympics. Forsaking lessons, the rope-tow and the beginners' slope, I rode the chair-lift confidently to the top of the mountain. Unbeknownst to me, skiers are expected to actually ski off the lift, transitioning from the moving lift to skiing down a man-made hill to clear the way for the next arriving pair of skiers. It was at this point that I realized just how tricky gravity could be, with a long pair of skis tethered to one's feet. My false bravado was exposed as I immediately allowed my skis to cross, ate a face-full of snow and created a massive logjam at the top of the hill. They were forced to stop the lift, get me untangled and separated from the mass of humanity coagulating at the summit, and moved safely out of everyone's way before returning to normal operating procedures. The only way I could have felt more stupid and self-conscious was if I had been skiing in my band uniform. My problems had just begun. It turns out that skiing is easy- well-waxed skis on a nearly frictionless surface makes skiing downhill a breeze- it's the maneuvering around objects like trees, snow-covered boulders and other skiers that's really the art. Oh, and stopping. The part about gravity that I failed to take into consideration was that whole thirty-two feet per second thing, which meant that gravity was pulling me downhill faster and faster until this skier, who had skipped the stopping lessons, simply fell down, repeatedly, about every fifty feet, all the way down the mountain. Actually, not all the way down. During one head-over-heels tumble a ski became untethered and rocketed down the slope like a missile, heat-seeking towards the fireplace in the ski lodge. Totally humiliated, I slung the other ski over my shoulder and walked the rest of the way down, avoiding the stares of the five- and six-year-olds who were fearlessly demonstrating how the sport was designed to be executed. I recovered the errant ski and walked over to the beginner slope. Having learned my lesson, I decided to take a lesson, all the while pondering the long bus ride home where it was likely that my friend would sit next to a skier. Oh well, I could spend the time reminiscing about the warmth of asphalt in August, and wondering if it was too late to rejoin the marching band.

GRACIE'S

"You know that look women get when they want to have sex?
Neither do I."

Trigger Warning: This great line by Steve Martin previews a funny but absolutely true vignette about sex and sex workers. Some may find this content to be offensive.

P erhaps it was the effect of two highly achieving older sisters entertaining their similarly high-achieving girlfriends at our house, but my problems, socially speaking, persisted through high school; once off to college, I determined to address the situation. There existed, across the Ohio River from our college campus, an establishment of young ladies under the tutelage of an older woman named Gracie. This establishment was popular with a certain class of men who found themselves frustrated for one reason or another and were willing to pay for female companionship to ease their frustration. One of the most frustrated subsets of men, certainly in the mid-sixties, were male college students, particularly those who had been drinking. Stories about this place circulated around the freshmen dormitories practically from the moment I set foot on campus. Remember, if you will, that this was 1966, in Appalachia, for crying out loud, then and still a very conservative place. The college, small and itself very conservative, had strict rules insofar as dating was concerned, including a 9:00 p.m. curfew except on Saturdays, date night, which I believe was midnight. History buffs may recall that this was before the "Summer of Love"; the Monterey Pop Festival, Haight-Ashbury and that

14

whole "Peace and Love" thing were off in the future and were going to unspool initially on the west coast, certainly not in Washington County, Ohio. Free love? As if. Conservative parents sent their daughters to a conservative college like this to protect them from the deviant social changes that were beginning to percolate beneath the surface of polite, repressed 1950's style society, after all. These parents may have appreciated an enterprise like Gracie's- a place where the young men dating their daughters could exhaust their animal urges before or after dropping them off at 9:00 pm. In any event, a couple of young college men who had been drinking, and who also happened to be my roommates, decided to make the trip across the river and somehow managed to talk me into it. Most college guys, liquored up, probably could not wait to make their first trip to a bordello. I, on the other hand, was ambivalent at best. Two older sisters? Check. Catholic school? Yup. Catholic guilt? In spades. We drove to West Virginia, strode purposefully to the door, knocked and listened to approaching footsteps. The moment of truth arrived. The door opened, Gracie checked us out and her gaze stopped at me and my long hair and issued her decree. "Boy, if you cain't afford a haircut, you cain't afford a piece of ass." Excuse me, Madam? I hadn't expected and couldn't process this rejection. You're saying I can't (cain't) pay one of your employees, whose job is literally to provide sex for money, to have sex with me? I wasn't even wearing that ridiculous band uniform.

Who would have suspected back then that my chances of having sex were better with a Catholic priest than with a paid professional? Oops, bad taste? In light of the evidence, I would argue that they have earned whatever derision is heaped upon them. This whole fiasco did have long-term consequences to my self-esteem, however, as I returned to campus ruminating about my epic, history-making failure to score under these circumstances.

WENDY'S

"Where's the Beef?"
A mid-80's advertising slogan used by the hamburger chain

W endy's and Gracie's have nothing in common, except, a cynic might argue, they are both "meat markets." Funny things may be true, but they are not necessarily laugh out loud humorous, sometimes they are simply quirky or memorably peculiar. One of my earliest interactions as a trucker has stuck with me for a very long time for this reason. I made a delivery in the early 1970's to someplace in Ohio- Akron or Dayton, I think it was. The load was restaurant furniture, and the consignee (truck talk for "who is getting the load and signing the freight bill") was a fast food franchise. Not a franchise exactly, not yet, but the person helping me unload the truck was Dave Thomas, and the restaurant was his second Wendy's location. This would have been another in a long series of forgettable deliveries were it not for the eventual success of the franchise and the monumentally absurd advice I remember offering to Mr. Thomas about his career choice. I said to him, to Dave Thomas you understand, "You can't make any money selling hamburgers. The big money is in trucking!" So, by the time I got my union withdrawal card in 1989, Dave Thomas, meat purveyor, had made me eat my words many millions of times. But wait, it gets better. Eventually, I transitioned into transportation safety and found myself working at Duke University in Durham, North Carolina, where, among other things, I taught monthly defensive driving classes to staff, students and contractors who drove Duke vehicles. I frequently had folks from the R. David Thomas Executive Conference Center attend these classes and through them I learned that this Center, an adjunct to the School of Business, was named in honor of my old friend Dave. Dave Thomas, who had dropped out of high school, endowed Duke with a sizeable enough gift from his "can't make any money" hamburger empire to get naming rights on a building. R. David Thomas was hamburger Dave. Okay, Dave, I'm sorry. Obviously, one can make a lot of money selling hamburgers, but enough already. I could use one of your 1260 calorie Triple Bacon Jalapeno Cheeseburgers right about now; it seems I've lost my appetite for humble pie.

THE MARINE

Hitchhiking was not a fad, but a viable means of travel for thousands of mostly young people in the '60s. I routinely hitchhiked to high school because my parents gave me bus money and, if I caught a ride, I could afford an extra slice of cafeteria pizza for lunch. There were a couple of teachers who would pick me up if they saw me, but the trip home was hit or miss. There was one woman who would stop when she saw me, and she earned the nickname "crazy lady" for her habit of goosing the accelerator–accelerate then brake, on-off, on-off, then on-off again so that the vehicle was propelled in an unending cycle of fits and starts. I alternated between being thrust backwards into the seat and then bowing forward at the waist as I tried to make conversation with her, which was unsettling, to say the least, but I was always happy to see her. After high school I continued the practice, sometimes bumming rides back and forth from my home in Connecticut to college in Ohio. My personal best was eleven hours door-to-door, which was great time for a trip of 600 miles. The worst? Twenty-six hours, after standing on the Pennsylvania Turnpike all night and then getting stuck on the Connecticut Turnpike for hours only twenty miles from home. Hitchhiking across Europe became a rite of passage for many young adults during summer vacations during that period, though I could not afford the luxury of a summer off from work. Although I met my share of weirdos and creeps in my travels, the practice was considered safe enough that it was not unusual to see plenty of young men and women making their way on the side of the road with their thumbs stuck out. One gentleman, a salesman most likely, would not let me into his car until I emptied out the contents of my duffel bag. At the time, I figured he was making sure that I didn't have a knife concealed in a hollowed-out textbook, but now, older, wiser and much more cynical, he may have wanted to see if I was a boxer or briefs kind of guy.

My brother purchased a Volkswagen bus from a college friend in North Carolina, and wanted me to accompany him south to retrieve it and share the drive back to Connecticut. The trip started well; we got picked up immediately and were driven to New York City. The problem was, our ride terminated in the Bronx near the George Washington Bridge, where our benefactor exited the interstate at the West Side Highway. Understanding that no one would stop in such a dangerous location, we started to hoof it around the burned-out vehicle carcasses and other detritus that defined the Cross-Bronx Expressway. We paused halfway across the bridge for a brief comfort stop into the Hudson River, then proceeded to the toll booths on the New Jersey side to try our luck there. Here's where it got interesting. Thumbs out and desperate for a ride in the middle of the craziness that is the toll plaza, we heard a loud-speaker barking out the order to "Stand down, hitchhikers, there is a trooper on his way to pick you up." This chilling command was emanating from a helicopter (you heard me correctly and no, we couldn't believe it either) and, as we looked around for the hopeful sign of other hitchhikers and seeing none, realized this directive was meant for us. Before the trooper could get to us, however, we scored a ride and figured we had managed a narrow escape. Unbeknownst to us as we celebrated our good fortune, we were being followed; we remain unsure if it was by helicopter or by the state trooper, but we were picked up immediately after our rescuer deposited us many exits later as he left the highway. Just think about the time, trouble and expense this took on the part of the state of

New Jersey to nab a couple of hitchhikers. On the ride to the police barracks in New Brunswick, the peace officer, performing his gruff, hard-as-nails role to the hilt, asked for identification, so I handed him my wallet. Tossing it back to me, he said that he couldn't take my f**king wallet, just hand him some f**king I.D. Sensing his effort to intimidate, I took out a gas credit card and passed it forward. He took one look at it and threw that over his shoulder into the back seat and said "Give me your goddam license. "Oh," I said, "why didn't you just ask for my license in the first place?" He was role-playing: the jack-booted Nazi cop playing rough with a couple of dirty hippies for whom he blamed the entire counterculture thing. When we got to the State Police barracks in New Brunswick where we were to be jailed until processed, he remained in character. I stopped in the corridor for a drink at the water fountain. "Don't drink that water!" he yelled, clearly relishing his role as the Obergruppenführer. And my reply, relishing my role as dirty, hippie irritant responded innocently "Why, is it non-potable?" A brief look of confusion and contempt crossed his countenance just before he put us in a cell and slammed the door shut. We shared the cell with another couple, a young Vietnam veteran and his fourteen-year-old brother who had also been picked up for hitchhiking. The younger brother had an attitude and refused to be pushed around. "Why aren't you out fighting crime instead of picking on innocent people?" he asked anyone who passed by. While we were waiting to be booked, he busied himself with locking all the leg irons(!) together and rattling the cell bars, swearing that he "...refused to eat this slop," although it was unlikely that food of any distinction would be forthcoming. After spending most of the morning waiting to be booked, we were finally hauled before a judge to post bond. Due to our lack of experience in these sorts of matters, we were both under the mistaken impression that we were paying a traffic fine and immediately forgot about it. Months later, as the two of us toiled away in a tomato cannery in Modesto, California, arrest warrants arrived at my parents' house in Connecticut (the address of record on our drivers' licenses). It seems that the fine we thought we had paid was actually a bond we had posted to appear in court, a court date we had missed, which made us wanted criminals. For hitchhiking. After court, we were escorted to the closest Greyhound terminal and put on a bus back to the Port Authority in New York City, where this ridiculous exercise had begun may hours earlier. Abandoning our quest, we eventually made it back to Connecticut where the trip south to pick up the VW bus would have to be temporarily postponed.

On one of my solo excursions west I got picked up outside of Wheeling, West Virginia, by a young guy about my age. My hair was shoulder-length and he was well-groomed and clean cut. You never knew what to expect when you hitched a ride, so, after the routine "Thanks for stopping" I usually deferred to the driver to start a conversation.

He began, "You a college student?"

"Yeh," I said, "I'm heading back to school. What do you do?" "I'm a Marine," he replied. "Really? How do you like it?" "It's not too bad," he answered, then he followed with, "What are you studying?" I told him I was majoring in psychology. "No kidding. I don't know much about psychology," he admitted, "but I know the Marines used it on me." Now he had my attention. "How so?" At that time, it was rumored that the government was conducting experiments on LSD; I expected him to tell me that he had been forced to perform as a lab rat for some bizarre CIA-funded study, but no. "When I finished basic training, I was convinced that I was the meanest, baddest motherfucker who ever lived. When I got my leave and came home, I went to a bar, got drunk and let everybody know just how tough I was."

"So…" I had to know, "what happened?"

"I got the shit kicked out me, that's what happened. And that's when I knew it was psychology." I spent four years in college and he got the same degree in an evening out. Semper Fi.

WOODSTOCK

"By the time we got to Woodstock, we were half a million strong..." Joni Mitchell

W hat can you say about the 1960s? There was so much going on in the late sixties that any number of funny things were true. Hair styles were funny, as were men's and women's fashion. Bell-bottom pants and collars out to our shoulders? Please, we looked like circus clowns, but maybe that was the point. The Merry Prankster, a communal group of hippies who traveled in a psychedelic painted school bus called Furthur, organizing parties and tripping on mind-expanding drugs, were role models, after all. It was not all fun and games, of course, as thousands of our contemporaries were being shipped to Southeast Asia to fight in a questionable and divisive conflict, so we had the "Generation Gap". Hawks versus Doves. I had a college friend whose brother was a defendant in the Chicago Seven trial (these were the seven defendants charged by the federal government with conspiracy and other charges related to anti-war protests that took place at the Democratic National Convention in 1968 in Chicago), so I joined the Students for a Democratic Society (SDS) chapter on campus, but, speaking frankly, it was less about staking out a political position than it was about making out in the missionary position. Solidarity? You bet, with the open-minded, progressive young women of "the Movement." Even so, the schismatic Culture Wars could have their moments, if you maintained the proper perspective. A popular Nixon era bumper sticker said "America- Love it or Leave It"; mine said "Humanity- Love it or Leave It". (This era ended ig-nominiously for Nixon on August 8, 1974, when he was forced to resign because, as it turned out, he *was* a crook. I was playing pool in a Eugene, Oregon roadhouse when the announcement was made. Above the din of cheering, clapping and whistling, free drinks were provided for all). Illegal herbs were rife and could make the mundane, like a flat tire, funny (see below*). I thought it was funny when my psychology professor asked me if I'd like to take a ride in his new Porche 911 Cabriolet. You bet I would. I was in my late teens- just coming down from the peak of my reckless, thrill-seeking, testosterone-fueled behavior. By this time, I had owned three motorcycles, each with more displacement and faster than the previous one. I had been cited for speeding on the New Jersey Turnpike for going… well, for narrative sake, let's just say for exceeding the speed limit. (Fortunately, this traffic stop occurred before the hitchhiking fiasco, or it's likely that I would have been hauled off and jailed for skipping out on my bond). So, yes, the idea of getting in a German sports convertible and letting it rip definitely appealed to my late teenaged self. As I anticipated, we got on the interstate and in no time at all we were over a hundred miles an hour. At this speed, Dr. L. leaned over and said "You don't seem impressed." Truth is, I *was* totally impressed- it was an awesome performance in a beautiful automobile; I was truly enjoying myself and had no intention of hurting his feelings when I observed, honestly, that when you've driven that fast on a motorcycle it doesn't feel so fast in a car. He slowed down, found an exit and dumped me back on campus.

1969 was an amazing summer. Music was definitely in the air. Living in Boston for the summer meant free concerts, particularly at the Boston Gardens, at the Hatch bandshell on the Charles River and on the Commons in Cambridge. My roommates and I went to clubs every weekend and welcomed the "British Invasion," the bands from England who were touring in the states. Jethro Tull and Ten Years After at the Boston Tea Party. Jeff Beck and Rod Stewart with about fifty other fans in a high school auditorium on the North Shore. The Moody Blues, prepared to offer their magnum opus, "Days of Future Passed" plugged in their synthesizer, blew the lights out and performed an acoustic set in a darkened venue. Most music though, was expected to be played loud. I attended a show by the band Mountain, featuring Long Island guitarist Leslie West, and lost my hearing for three days. I saw Led Zeppelin three times that summer, once opening for Jose Feliciano (we arrived late and asked the ticket taker if we had missed anything. He told us not to worry, the opening act wasn't any good. Led Zeppelin is in the Rock and Roll Hall of Fame, but hey, "Feliz Navidad" is a pretty rocking tune as well) and once for Frank Zappa and The Mothers of Invention. I hit the trifecta when I saw Cream, as it completed a fantasy trio of ex-Yardbirds guitarists-Eric Clapton, Jeff Beck and Jimmy Page in one summer. The night I saw Blood, Sweat and Tears perform, I struck up a conversation with Jerry Hyman, their trombone player, and we went out for a beer afterwards. As we walked into a local dive, the mostly working-class clientele looked at our long hair with scorn, but Jerry introduced himself and mentioned that his band had a big hit called "You Made Me So Very Happy," that was getting a lot of airtime on the radio and was available on their juke box. Offering to play this immediately recognizable song for them, he put coins in the machine and proceeded to punch the wrong buttons. We were briefly entertained by some dreadful tune that left them so very unhappy; we finished our beers and left.

Trivia buffs may remember Mitch Ryder and the Detroit Wheels ("Devil with the Blue Dress" was probably their biggest hit). I took a date to see him perform and she finagled an invitation to his afterparty at the hotel. We arrived on my motorcycle as Mitch was getting out of his limo; he saw the bike and asked me if he could take it for a ride. I said sure, why not? Coincidentally, two of his songs were "Jenny Take a Ride" and "C.C. Rider". As far as I can discern, neither song was about motorcycles; in any event, my date (whose name was not Jenny, nor was she wearing a blue dress) hopped on the back and off they went. They weren't gone long, or long enough for concern, that is, or else this might have qualified as a "funny business is true" episode. (I either had great taste in motorcycles or lousy taste in women, as this very same thing happened again a couple of years later. This time it was my roommate who borrowed my bike and my date, and disappeared for about twenty-four hours, which, of course, triggered this old joke: My live-in girlfriend had disappeared for a couple of days, so I called the police. They told me that the first 24 hours were the most critical; if I hadn't heard from her, I should probably plan for the worst. With this in mind, I drove to the Salvation Army store to see if I could buy her clothes back). If you remember Mr. Ryder, you may recall some of the lesser-known bands from that period, and the difficulty they had coming up with original names. Vanilla Fudge begat Strawberry Alarm Clock. What, no chocolate-flavored music? How about the Electric Prunes? (Sounds more like a dietary supplement for aging Baby Boomers).

The modern equivalent for the lack of band-naming creativity would be the current hip-hop fashion of substituting the letter "z" for "s." Its rap-rehensible ubiquity screams "Don't listen to our music! We sound exactly like everyone else!" Speaking as a COP (Certified Old Person) they do sound exactly like everyone else. ZZ Top gets a pass, but seriously, the last person who managed to pull the "Z" thing off with panache was Don Diego de la Vega.

The Newport Jazz Festival was held in early July, a short drive from Boston; later that month men landed on the moon. Hippies descended upon Bethel, New York, by the (Volkswagen) bus load for the Woodstock Festival, in August. I was loading trucks for UPS that summer when my roommates and I sent away for tickets (which I still have, by the way. I'd be willing to guess that their nostalgic value makes them worth more now than their eighteen-dollar face price).

Tickets to the 1969 Woodstock Music and Art Fair

The festival was scheduled to run from Friday, August 15th through Sunday, the 17th. We packed camping gear and left Boston after work on Thursday, get this, to beat the crowd. Somewhere in the Berkshires we heard a strange thumping noise and ignored it until we realized it was a flat tire. (*We laughed). After changing the tire, we resumed our trip to ensure that we would get "good seats." When we arrived at the festival site, we were still about five miles from the stage location in a massive traffic jam, created by everyone else who had left home early in order to get good seats. We pulled off the road and set up our tents, rolled out our sleeping bags and went to sleep.

Friday was Folk day. The opening act was Ritchie Havens, followed by folk music heavyweights including Joan Baez, Tim Hardin, and John Sebastian. It was a beautiful late summer evening; the weather was perfect and I was in repose, eyes closed, enjoying the music when I heard a familiar voice. "Hey, asshole, what are you doing here?" It was my brother, just graduated from high school, so I said, "What do you mean 'What am I doing here,' What are *you* doing here?" His answer threw me. "I'm going to get a cup of coffee" he said. Wait, what? I don't know what I was expecting- seeking enlightenment, perhaps? Grooving on the peace and love thing maybe? The notorious brown acid, maybe, but not the benign brown caffeinated liquid; coffee was not on the list. "No, I mean how did you talk Mom and Dad into letting you come to this?" The parents, it turns out, were off on vacation somewhere so my brother and a friend jumped in a car and drove to New York. What amazes me now (or, considering the reference: What blows my mind...) was that, on a hillside in a sea of people numbering nearly a half-million, his meandering path for "a cup of coffee" took him right past my blanket. We chatted briefly and parted with the obligatory "See you later." I did not run into him again at the festival. In fact, we did not see each other again until Thanksgiving, since I returned to Boston and then, weeks later, went back to school. He was also off to college that fall, so it was months before we crossed paths again. Believe it or not, a bizarrely similar set of circumstances would unfold years later while my wife and I were on vacation in Ireland. Our younger son was finishing a semester abroad at University College, Cork, and we had booked a tour to see Ireland before meeting him at school to pack up his things and bring him home. His older brother had flown over; the two of them planned a walkabout when exams were completed, to do some hiking and camping before meeting the parents back in Cork. We would gather there and fly home together. One afternoon, our coach operator unloaded us at our hotel in Killarney; we checked in and decided to find a pub and enjoy a stout. As we set off from the hotel, my wife remarked how weird it would be if we ran into our boys, who had no itinerary and were basically just bumming around the country on their way south to Cork. Minutes later that I poked her and said, "Guess what?" Travis, who is nearly 6'7" and was sporting a wild red afro at the time, was towering over everyone else in the approaching crowd. Killarney has a population of about 14,500 people, tiny compared to Woodstock that weekend, but still, in the middle of Ireland (population 4.9

million, about ten times the population in Woodstock for the festival) what were the odds? I can report that they were sincerely happy to see us, since this meant a hot shower and a good meal for them for the first time in days.

GRADUATE SCHOOL

G etting into college has never been easier. It is easier, after all, to research schools and schedule admission interviews online than to make campus visits. Marginal students have been known to pay a genius friend to take the SATs for them, and wealthy parents still face the shame of getting caught bribing a school official. (Or bribing a doctor: in the uber-wealthy town of Greenwich, Connecticut, where students are already gifted with a plenitude of academic advantages, fifty per cent of them are allowed to take the SATs without time limits due to cognitive disabilities attested to by family doctors). Back in my day we had to walk eight miles through two feet of snow just to fill out an application. And, I should add, the "Boomer Bulge" made getting into college much more competitive back then, since the huge middle class created in postwar America (fueled, in no small part, by labor unions. In the 1950's, one worker out of three was represented by a union; today the number has shrunk to one out of ten) meant many more first-time college attendees competing for acceptances. Now though, having been out of school and in the job market for a couple of years, I began to reflect how easy I had had it as a student; late nights at the pub were easier to take than late nights on dark highways. Therefore, when a friend mentioned that he had been accepted to graduate school in Tennessee, and that he needed a roommate for two years, I applied. Weeks later I was surprised with an acceptance letter and made plans to visit the campus and make living arrangements for the fall semester. The wise thing to do, it turns out, would have been to make a visit before applying, particularly since my friend had backed out and I would now be flying solo. I arrived in town in midsummer and began my tour of the city- in reality, a smallish burg in eastern Tennessee. It had been a long drive and I thought a cold beer would help me unwind enough to begin my search for housing. I stopped at a grocery store, parked my car (adorned with its Connecticut license plates) and went inside. As I walked up and down the aisles searching for beer, a friendly crazy person masquerading as a grocery store employee approached and asked if I needed assistance; I affirmed my intention to buy some brew. His response that I was now in the bible belt and the sale of beer was illegal threw me momentarily, but I recovered quickly and maybe a tad injudiciously. "Wow. No beer, huh?" Can you point me to the wine aisle then; I know they drank that in the bible. The wedding feast at Cana, you might remember, was Jesus' first public miracle. Turning water into wine was a great party trick, that, and a fairly terrific wedding gift." A lot of good that Catholic school education did for me, as this young clerk did not appear overly impressed with my knowledge of the New Testament. Instead, he might have thought me subversive as he ran to the nearest telephone, because I barely had time to return to my car, empty handed, and head towards campus when I noticed flashing police lights in my rearview mirror. Pulled over, license and registration and the third degree. After offering a fairly lengthy and detailed biography, the peace officer asked me where I was staying. "As I said two or three times, I'm a prospective student looking for an apartment for the fall term."

"So," he calculated, "you don't have an address locally?"

"No sir, not until you let me go and I have the opportunity to find a place." He pulled his ace card. "I could arrest you for vagrancy, you know. Being that you don't have a place to stay."

"Yes, but by that logic I'm sure most graduate students arriving at school would be considered vagrants and you couldn't possibly arrest the entire entering class. If you let me go, I can find a place to live and then everyone wins."

"All right, I'll let you go this time."

"Thank you, sir. Have a nice day."

I was beginning to have doubts about my near-term goals. To make a long, boring story short and boring, I got pulled over a couple more times before dark, including a second time by the same cop. In addition to being dry, this county had another quasi-legal ripple that I was not aware of, and that was the extremely brief window of time they gave outsiders (from the northeast?) to sign a lease. These peace officers were letting me know, in their quaint southern way, that I was perilously close to violating their grace period. Exasperated, I finally explained that, with their frequent interruptions, they were only delaying my search to find a place to live and I would be more productive if they left me alone. Wrong answer, obviously, but the story ended well, nevertheless. You see, I found great accommodations for my one-night stay, and the price fit my budget. My hosts at the county jail refused to provide me breakfast, but this was also a positive development, as it hastened my exit from town. As a bonus, their hospitality put me back in the job market and saved me two years of tuition payments. And, lastly, as I ruminated on the long drive home, it explained why I had received my acceptance letter so quickly- who else in their right mind would ever apply to a place where the locals drove you to drink? In the next county.

THE TONIGHT SHOW

One question I was frequently asked was "Don't you ever get bored driving a truck?" The honest answer should have been, yes, of course. Come on, have you ever driven across Nebraska? The topography of Nebraska may be sleep-inducing, but even that remote environment could generate the occasional funny but true anecdote. For example: my brother and I were driving to California in his VW microbus, its 48-horsepower engine chugging along nicely until all of a sudden it wasn't, and we were dead on the side of the road. We had no tools, no spare parts, and no clue why the engine had ceased functioning, but were greatly heartened when a pick-up truck, towing an impressively long trailer, stopped and two cowboys got out (we assumed they were cowboys because of their cowboy hats and cowboy boots, the belt buckles and, you know, that whole cowboy demeanor) and walked up to the van. They asked what happened; we explained the situation and were mightily relieved when they described themselves as mechanics and offered to take a look. They walked behind the bus, lifted the engine cover and laughed out loud as they saw the tiny lawn-mower-looking motor that sat in the engine compartment. "Well, boys," they explained, "we're actually jet engine mechanics. This here (pointing to their impressively long trailer) is the fastest car in the world, (Gary Gabelich, driving his car the "Blue Flame" had set the land-speed record- 622.407 miles per hour- in October the previous year) and we're on our way to the Bonneville Salt Flats for some testing. (Dang! At that speed we could have driven from Connecticut to California in under five hours)! Sorry, but other than taking you down the road so you can call a tow truck, we don't think we can help." The call was made and the tow truck eventually arrived, hooked up to the van, pulled on to the interstate and promptly quit. A second tow truck was called. We managed to record this humiliation on film, but the photographer, a friend of my brother's who was accompanying us on the trip, fumbled her camera and dropped it into a Nebraska irrigation ditch. Thus, our classic photo of a tow truck towing a tow truck towing a Volkswagen van was immediately and irretrievably lost to posterity. We finally made it to the nearest exit in Cozad, Nebraska, where we spent a lovely weekend, waiting for a service station to reopen after a long fourth of July holiday. Okay, maybe not so funny at the time, but still...

The same landscape, endlessly, and mile after mile of corn fields between exits *can* get boring, but I would usually answer the question, "Not at all. I really enjoy the pleasure of my own company." And, for the most part I was capable of entertaining myself. I listened to whatever music I could find on the radio, which informed my musical taste; I still maintain an eclectic mix of genres. Don't forget, I had been weaned on the music of my parents' tastes- big band, swing and jazz, and had been exposed to classical music while performing in band and orchestra, so I composed song lyrics in my head to pass the time. Sample:

"Bury Me in My Peterbilt"

When I was only half my age, I just turned twenty-six,
My uncle had me in his rig, split-shifting those twin sticks.
My boots could barely reach the floor, I hadn't drunk a beer,
But, Lord, he cussed like hell whene'er I missed a gear.

Well, all those times have changed by now, I'm older, more mature,
And now my own rig knows her way from Bangor to Ventura,
And though I run from coast to coast I'll always have a home,
'Cause home is where my heart is, and my heart is where I roam.

So, bury me in my Peterbilt when I'm dead and gone,

'Cause when you've spent a life like mine, it's the only life I've known.
I've never been alone, not once, and if you ask me why
I'm with my friend, my only friend ,
at that Truck Stop in the sky.

Somewhere along the road of life, the signs all say "Go Slow"',
And at that time there's no denyin' your life's ebb starts to flow.
I know one day I'll see those signs and know my time is near,
I'll head straight for those Pearly Gates that say "Trucks Enter Here."

You get the idea. A simple exercise to pass the time and keep myself awake and, before I knew it, I would be crossing the state line into Wyoming.

Citizen Band (CB) radios did not keep me much entertained in the early days because they were few and far between when I started driving and it was mostly dead air on every channel. It wasn't until C.W. McCall wrote a 1975 song about a convoy of truckers that they became de rigueur for big rigs, and a 1978 movie based on the song made them ubiquitous in four-wheelers (passenger vehicles). The truth is, I rarely turned my CB radio on because... well, because I preferred the solitude of my own company and the entertaining voices in my head to the inane chatter of a multitude of trucker wannabees speaking in 10-code. I preferred dead air.

If you think back to that era, to the era of CB radios, you may remember the Tonight Show with Johnny Carson. Conventional wisdom had it that a spot on the Tonight Show could make a career, so obviously, that became my goal. The problem was that I had no talent, no skills, no career to make, really; I had nothing except a fairly wide-ranging imagination that kept me occupied to stave off boredom. I did recognize, though, a platform for self-promotion in the form of all of those trucks traveling coast to coast. Thus, a plan was hatched. My plan was to print thousands of bumper stickers that said "I've Met Chris Wardell- Have You?"

and affix them to every trailer in every truck stop I visited. Eventually someone would have to ask, "I saw that bumper sticker in Idaho last week. Who is that guy?" and I would be ready for Johnny with my killer song lyrics. Or something. Let's draw a couple of conclusions. Conclusion #1: You've never heard of me, because, conclusion #2: I never printed thousands of bumper stickers. As it happened, I did share this fantasy with a friend of mine and she surprised me one birthday with a handful of these bumper stickers that she had had printed. Maybe I never appeared on television, and fame clearly eluded me, but a few of those stickers did find their way onto a mélange of guitar cases and car bumpers owned by friends who had more loyalty than taste. In fact, my brother reminded me that he had one on his car that made a subsequent journey to the left coast, so there is a chance that it may have been seen and afforded me some very minor celebrity after all.

ROAD TRIP

A Texan on vacation takes a road trip to Wisconsin. Spotting a fellow farmer repairing a fence near the road, he stops to chat. "What do you grow?" he asks. "Nothin', really" is the reply, "it's a dairy farm. I graze cows on my land." "Listen," the vacationer brags. "Back in Texas I can hop in my truck and drive all day, all night and most of the next day and still be on my property." "Tell me about it," commiserated the dairy farmer. "I owned a truck like that once."

My wife, (my girlfriend, still, at that moment in time), accompanied me on a six-hundred-mile trip in my early trucking days. The trucks were somewhat primitive in those days- fairly utilitarian boxes mounted on a chassis over the engine. These were called cabover trucks, identifiable by a flat front like the old Volkswagen buses and they were popular on the east coast because of overall length restrictions. These restrictions were state-by-state regulatory limits on the allowable "combination length" of a truck-tractor pulling a trailer, and they were considerably less liberal in the eastern United States than those in the "wide open spaces" out west. As you drove west, one saw more conventional trucks, or trucks whose engines were out in front of the cab, with long hoods to accommodate the bigger engines these trucks required for driving in the mountains.

Wardell Family Archives

This COE (cab over engine) had great visibility but little else to recommend it.

The difference was more than aesthetic, though, since conventional trucks were smoother riding due to their spread-out wheelbases. I impart this information to the reader for the same reason I explained it to my girlfriend- this truck was noisy (because we were sitting on top of the engine) and hot (because, ditto) and uncomfortable. I told her that I doubted if she would be able to fall asleep as she got bounced around behind me in the sleeper berth. When I first started trucking with a co-driving partner, I had been unable to sleep for three straight days until I got used to the noise and vibrations. (There was a bumper sticker sold in Pennsylvania truck stops at that time that said, "Pray for Me- I Drive I-80). I recall that she made it about ninety miles sitting up front with me; once we made it through New York City she climbed in back to sleep. "This should be interesting," I thought, wondering how far she would make it before giving up. That question was answered a mere eight hours later when she poked her head out from behind the curtain and asserted that she had just had the best sleep ever. My wife: confounding me since 1973. (Insert joke, apropos of nothing in particular except that it relates to driving down the highway in a truck with my wife, here: Remember the Bobbitts? The husband, John, routinely beat his wife, Lorena, and she finally retaliated by cutting off his penis while he slept. Not funny, but absolutely true, you can look it up. Okay, picture this. Instead of doing it while he slept, she cuts it off while they're driving down the road and tosses it out the window. It hits the windshield and my wife, who is my girlfriend at the time, looks at me in amazement, and says, "Did you see the size of the penis on that bug?")

Wardell Family Archives
The truck illustrated here is a conventional, with the engine out in front of the cab.

Many years later, I asked my nine-year-old son if he would be interested in taking a ride with me in the truck. I had a short overnight trip planned to deliver a truck to a customer in New Jersey and then to head to a dealer in upstate New York to pick up a unit that was being brought back to our shop in Connecticut. I would be using a lowboy trailer for this trip, and I thought he would enjoy the view from way up in the passenger seat. He was excited to make the trip with me and packed a suitcase full of books, toys and puzzles to keep himself entertained. Before we hit the highway, though, he had climbed into the sleeper berth and emptied his cache of trucks and cars and busied himself in make-believe trucking. "Wouldn't you like to come up here and see what it looks like from this height?" Maybe in a little while, he offered. He spent most of the day in back and rarely emerged until dinner time. I took him to an excellent restaurant I had found on a previous trip to Syracuse, and told him he could order anything on the menu. His eyes lit up, the waiter came and he placed his order for twin lobsters. There was no objection from me, since I was also a huge lobster fan (Literally. One time my wife and I cooked a twenty-two pound lobster. That was a huge lobster!) and anticipated finishing his leftovers. There were no leftovers, and somehow, after a day in the sleeper berth, he had managed to work up enough appetite for dessert.

The problem was, I have two sons and they differ in age by five years; I was out of the truck-driving business by the time the younger one was old enough to accompany me on a trip. After college he moved to New Zealand to find work and to travel, and from there he moved to China for a spell, and then to Vietnam. When he had concluded his adventures in that hemisphere, he called home and asked me if I would pick him up at the airport. "Of course, you don't even have to ask," I said, thrilled at the opportunity to see him again after a very long absence. "In Los Angeles?" he asked. I wasn't sure I understood him. "You need a ride from LAX?" "Hey," he replied. "You owe me a road trip." It was only too true- I did owe him a trip, and, because I had just exercised an early retirement option, I had plenty of free time. So, I bought a car on-line from a dealer in Los Angeles and asked them to pick me up at the airport, arranged a flight that would sync with my son's incoming flight from Asia and met him at baggage claim. He asked me where the car was and I told him that I hoped it was outside, because it was a long walk home. We walked out of the terminal, tracked down the salesperson and went back to the dealership to complete the paperwork, got in the car and headed east. The first night we made it to the Grand Canyon, where it was too dark to do any sightseeing, but early enough to watch our hometown Durham Bulls minor league baseball team win the Triple A League World Series on television. He and I then spent a leisurely three weeks on a road trip home to North Carolina while he regaled me with his far-flung travel experiences. It wasn't in a truck, but that was not really the point of the trip.

TYING THE KNOT

I was a couple of months shy of thirty when I got married and had spent a long time searching for Miss Right. She had a number of endearing nicknames while we dated; it wasn't until after I saw the marriage license that I realized her real first name was Always.

I mentioned my summer jobs working as a Teamster, but my career as a driver really got into gear after college as a long-haul trucker, running over-the-road, and getting home infrequently. In the course of my driving career I drove enough varied equipment that it's easier to mention what I didn't drive- fire engines and concrete mixers. I drove a garbage truck one summer during college. I hauled general freight in dry vans. I hauled frozen food in refrigerated trailers (reefers). I hauled steel, copper and aluminum, plywood and lumber on flatbeds. I hauled containers. I hauled heavy equipment on lowboys and drop-deck trailers. I worked construction for five years driving trailer-dump trucks, hauling asphalt, sand and gravel, all the while enjoying the luxury of fairly regular hours, Mondays through Fridays. Mostly, I hauled ass.

Here's a math problem: two trucks leave a truck stop together but travel in opposite directions. One truck heads east at fifty-five miles per hour and the other travels west at seventy-five mph. After how many hours will they be 520 miles apart? Examples like these are called Rate-Time-Distance problems and this formula: (rate multiplied by time equals distance), and vexing little problems like these may have accounted for the full employment of shop teachers in high schools across America. There may not be a surfeit of math majors driving big rigs over the road but every driver I ever met understood the ramifications of this simple formula: the driver heading west was making more money. Paying long-haul drivers by the mile may be standard industry practice, but the uncomfortable truth is that this encourages multiple unsafe behaviors. First and foremost, this practice rewards speeding. Higher speeds mean more miles and more miles mean bigger paychecks. Thus, it was not unusual for drivers to carry licenses from multiple states; this made it possible to accumulate speeding points on separate licenses, thus reducing the risk of forfeiture. Even I had a couple- one from my home state and one from Ohio, where I had gone to college. Some states had reciprocity agreements with their neighbors, but without a national database, checking a driver's status was time-consuming and labor-intensive. This problem was largely resolved in the 1980's by the creation of a national database and standardized regulations for Commercial Driver's License (CDL) holders. Until then, licenses issued by the states had different sets of qualification and renewal criteria. Following is an actual exchange that occurred before the standardization of Commercial Drivers' Licenses: I got pulled over, the cop looked at my license and asked me who gave me permission to drive the truck. Connecticut licenses were either Class 1, Class 2 or Class 3, similar to the current standard (Classes A, B, or C), and the differences were explained on the back, but he needed some help deciphering the Connecticut nomenclature. To ensure that I understood him, I repeated his question. "You're asking me who gave me permission to drive this truck?"

"Yes," he answered, "I want to know who gave you permission to operate this vehicle?"

It was clear to me that he wanted to know by what authority I was operating a Class 1 vehicle (duh, the Connecticut Department of Motor Vehicle, by issuance of the document he was holding in his hand) but since he lacked the ability to correctly phrase the question, I decided to play along.

"Frank," I answered.

"Say what?"

"You asked me who gave me permission to drive the truck

and I said Frank. Frank gave me permission to drive it. It's his truck." Okay, I was being a wise guy but I was annoyed that I had been stopped. We eventually got it straightened out and I was rolling again, with Frank's okay.

The second and only slightly less obvious result of this compensation practice is that it encourages operators to drive excessively long hours, since more time behind the wheel also means more miles accrued. Many drivers used to carry multiple log books (or joke books, or comic books, depending on the local vernacular); most large fleets now use on-board computers to monitor these metrics but cheating still abounds. As a former driver and as a safety advocate I understand and promote the logic of keeping tired drivers off the road, particularly after studies demonstrated that sleep-deprived drivers operate at the same increased risk of accidents as those who are impaired. It's the arbitrariness of it that rankles. Look, an employee, any employee in any industry, who has worked a long shift may get home, put his family in the car and head to Disney World. How is that any less dangerous than a trucker driving in excess of eleven hours (the present daily limit)? The reality is that cars cause eighty per cent of car-truck accidents, and aggressive, and/or impaired, and/or sleep-deprived four-wheelers account for most of these. Did you know that commercial drivers are required to be medically qualified and must pass a physical, including an eye exam, every two years? Did you know that drivers over a certain Body Mass Index (BMI) must submit to a sleep study to indicate the likelihood of sleep apnea? High blood pressure or insulin dependence will put a trucker out of service. Did you know that commercial drivers must pass a pre-employment drug screen, and, once hired, submit to random, post-accident and reasonable-suspicion drug tests? In most circumstances, an automobile driver who gets a license at sixteen can renew that license until death with no additional testing. The truth is, there is no "one size fits all" when it comes to time-off requirements, because all humans do not require the same amount of sleep. And, by the way, parking freight for ten hours (the mandatory down-time between driving shifts) may improve the bottom-line of the truck stop but does little to "Keep America Moving." Hence the appeal of team operations. Two operators sharing the driving can keep the truck rolling, and the miles accruing, without running into regulatory hell.

In the midst of all this math mumbo-jumbo (by the way, the answer to our rate x time= distance problem is four hours) and all this hauling, I managed a life outside of work. And given my idiosyncratic nature and the circumstances of my work, it was a fairly normal life. I met a young woman and we shared a life for five years before I eventually asked her to marry me. You might think the circumstances of my proposal were funny but true, or you might just think I'm a jerk, but both things could be true. After living together for five years, she got tired of my failure to commit (what, five years isn't a commitment?) and moved into her own apartment. We didn't really see each other any less, but she had stated her case and made her position clear. I was forced to consider long-term circumstances, and knew a proposal was inevitable, but, me being me, it had to be made in a face-saving manner.

I had grown up as a rabid New York Giants football fan, and now they were mired in a generational long streak of mediocrity. In the early seventies I had even managed to attend a number of their "home" games as a result of the renovation of Yankee Stadium, their actual home field. In 1973 and 1974 they played 12 home games at the Yale Bowl, home to the Yale University football team in New Haven, Connecticut. Anyway, one of their biggest rivals was the Washington Redskins, who were beating them soundly on this particular Sunday. She asked me again why I wouldn't commit to her and respecting her position I offered the following- "Look, if the Giants pull this game out, we can get married." I've retold this story many times, usually framed in terms of a bet which I lost, but I'm fairly certain that I was hoping the Giants would win because, 1) I would never have rooted against them, and 2) I would have managed to propose without the humiliation of actually making a proposal (or, to use football terminology, "taking a knee"). It turns out to have been my good fortune that the Giants did manage a late field goal to come from behind and, before the clock expired, she had called family and friends to inform them that I had *proposed* and we were getting married. I won't say that I was reluctant to tie the knot once I made the offer in January, but I did put the date off as far as I possibly could- the last day of the year, New Year's Eve. Fate, as is its habit, intervened.

There are a million in-law jokes. But I was particular; I had shopped for a family, not just a bride; my relationship with her family was based as much on love and trust for them as it was for her. They were unique and interesting, but even better, they were quirky. I could be myself around them, because these were qualities we shared and they accepted in me. So, on Saint Patrick's Day, March 17th, when my prospective father-in-law went in for a routine pre-surgical checkup, we were still planning a big wedding for the end of December. When he returned hours later with a cancer diagnosis, and a prognosis of six to eight weeks to live, we switched into overdrive.

A short biography about my father-in-law might help. If I was asked to describe him in a single word, I'm not sure which word I would choose. Smart? Clearly. He had received his Phi Beta Kappa key his junior year at Williams College and then graduated second in his class from Yale Law School. Interesting? To me, absolutely. Recruited for the CIA out of law school, he had taken his young family to Indochina to assist the French who were on the verge of getting run out of Vietnam. My wife had learned to speak Thai and Chinese before she could speak English. Funny? Most definitely, and one of his most endearing traits- the one bond we had that cemented our relationship. We shared a sense of humor that was a bit off-kilter, so it seemed sometimes that we were the only two laughing. Successful? By any measure. He had returned from the CIA and joined the law practice of his good friend who had finished first in the same class at Yale. Finding the practice of law not to his liking he joined the administration of Connecticut

Governor John Dempsey as a speechwriter and remained in state politics for the rest of his life. He was rewarded for this public service with a judicial appointment, and in 1978, after receiving his cancer prognosis, in lieu of our planned church ceremony, I asked him if he would marry the two of us in his capacity as a judge. (Let me vent, again, about the hypocrisy of the Catholic church. Our decision to have him marry us in a civil ceremony set off a series of events that might be described as funny but true, given the benefit of hindsight and once the whole story is told. The church got wind of our plans and threatened to excommunicate my father-in-law for marrying us outside of the church. True, but not funny. My wife had gone to the same Catholic grammar school as me, and, coincidentally, the same public high school, although we did not meet until we were both in our twenties. Remember, if you will, that my father-in-law had just received the equivalent of a death sentence, and wanted to make everything right with his Maker, so this news was not well-received. We assured him that we could make everyone happy; he need not worry. You see, we had a friend, a long-time drinking buddy actually, who had become a Dominican priest and was studying at the Yale Divinity School. We asked him if he could marry us in the Catholic church on Yale's campus and he agreed, so we met there in our beach attire, (he had his bathing suit on, under his robes, as he planned to accompany us to the afterparty), grabbed a couple of witnesses and did the "I do's." The funny part, from my perspective, is our friend the priest subsequently got his girlfriend pregnant and was forced to leave the church. You might say he "did the right thing" by marrying this woman, even though he ended up divorcing her and remarrying another woman a few years later. So, the church disavowed our civil ceremony but gave its imprimatur to a church-sanctioned sacrament conducted by a priest who ended up divorced, and twice-married. My wife and I honor this hypocrisy annually, by the way, by celebrating our anniversary on the date of our "real" wedding, conducted by a judge). Remember, we thought we had two months, maximum, to pull this off. The first thing I did was secure a venue. This was not as difficult as I anticipated because of the great goodwill of friends. There was, in my hometown, an excellent restaurant with a wonderful bar where we ate occasionally and drank frequently. The folks who ran the bar were the daughter of the proprietor and her husband who knew us well from our frequent visits. I inquired if there was a night within the six-to-eight-week window available when we could rent the bar for a reception and they said whatever night we wanted we could have. Date chosen; site secured. The next item on the list was to send the invitations. Initially, we had planned a big wedding reception/New Year's Eve party so we had to pare down the list considerably. This was not so difficult because if she and I eliminated work-related guests and focused on family and close friends the list became manageable. Alright then, the list was pared but now the real drama began- how to word the invitations. My father-in-law had not been a judge for long and remained enchanted with the trappings of his office. "Let me see," he began. "How should the invitation read? Judge and Mrs. Phillips? The Honorable Mr. and Mrs. Phillips?" I cut to the chase. "You'll need to come to a decision soon. If you continue to dither it will be the late Judge and Mrs. Phillips." There was the briefest of pauses as the rest of the family stopped breathing before he erupted into laughter. "Okay, Judge and Mrs. Phillips it is."

To this day, the memory of our wedding event is bittersweet. I believe it was helpful to all of us to have this wedding tumult going on, even as my father-in-law began his treatments and started preparing for his demise. At one point he seemed a bit low, so I suggested that he better really be dying and not merely faking a terminal illness just to marry off his daughter; if so, I would never forgive him. As I suspected, this amused him. He had a remarkable ability to laugh and, despite his brilliance, to laugh at himself. I've never met anyone who seemed so prepared to die in spite of the long life he must have thought he had in front of him. He was fond of reminding me that life itself was a terminal illness of uncertain duration. His was a too few fifty-six years.

COUPE DE VILLE

My wife and I inherited a wonderful old Chevy Biscayne from my in-laws after my sister-in-law had finished with it. She had used this vehicle as her commuter car during college, and by commute, I mean she had taken the car back and forth to Williamstown, Massachusetts, when she travelled for school holidays. While at school the car essentially sat in a remote parking lot buried under snow. I'm comfortable making that claim because Williamstown, located in the Berkshire mountains, averages sixty-three inches, or over five feet, of snow, every winter. And, because the average *annual* temperature in Williamstown is a fraction above forty-six degrees, and because she returned home for the warm months of summer, the snow was not of a mind to melt. So, by the time my wife and I took possession of this car it was twenty years old and, to use a descriptive automotive expression, had been around the block a time or two.

The Biscayne model by Chevrolet was their base model in the large sedan configuration. Younger readers probably cannot remember a time when vehicles were not equipped with all the amenities of a luxury home- reclining leather bucket seats, air-conditioning, multi-speaker stereos, power-everything and more computer brain power than Apollo 11. (Younger readers probably cannot remember Apollo 11). When I describe this vehicle as a base model, I mean basic transportation – a small engine, a standard three-speed transmission (with a clutch and the gear shift on the steering column), roll-up windows, no radio, no carpeting, no kidding. The flooring was a thin rubber mat over a base of fibrous manila hemp. Basic, yes, but a welcome addition to a young family with a new baby. I drove this car; my wife used the car with the baby seat.

One afternoon I was driving home from work and I started to feel very warm. Understand that warmth was the natural habitat in this car, particularly in the late summer, so initially I thought the car was overheating. The gauges said no. The next sensation I felt was burning feet- they were not warm, but hot, so hot that I pulled over. Safely off the highway, and well over on the shoulder, I got out of the car and felt the floor beneath my feet. Something was wrong, so I investigated. I peeled the rubber mat back and, in the same instant that I noticed the highway shoulder where the car floor should have been, oxygen fed the small fire that had begun in the hemp mat (from direct contact with the extremely hot exhaust system) and my car became a flaming road-side attraction. If I had paid attention, I might have noticed piles of rust where I parked the car, but I suspect it was more likely that the car slowly disintegrated, mile by uncomfortable mile, as the car bounced along on twenty-year-old shock absorbers.

So, in the fall of 1983 and still shopping for a replacement vehicle, my delivery schedule had me periodically in eastern Connecticut. As such, I had the occasion to pass the Holy Trinity Greek Orthodox Church in Norwich once a week or so, and, parked on the lawn outside the church was a very handsome new Cadillac with a "Win This Car" banner affixed to the windshield. I'm not a gambler, but I did need a car and this was a church fundraiser, after all. My arguments against gambling were sound; the odds of winning are always skewed against you, and I worked too hard for my money to give it away. But, every time I drove by this car, I rationalized a bit more. On the plus side, they were limiting ticket sales to one hundred and fifty, so my odds were only one hundred and fifty to one. Not great- even a coin toss is a 50-50 proposition, but I did need a car. On the minus side, the tickets were one hundred and fifty dollars each, but, you know, I needed a car. I vacillated like this for weeks, until I decided to go for broke (there is a good reason this expression describes a gamble). The day of reckoning was nearing and I was afraid of missing the opportunity to own a Cadillac for one hundred and fifty dollars. Oddly, I had convinced myself that I had to take a chance because I could not abide some stranger winning "my car." I pulled the truck over and went inside. I found the church office and told the priest why I was there. "I only have two tickets left," he informed me, "and one of them is saved for someone stopping by later to pick it up." With that, he pulled both tickets out of the drawer and handed me one- the last ticket available. I gladly made the exchange for cash, because it was a church fundraiser, you recall, and I was convinced that he had just handed me the title to a new Cadillac. I thanked him and left. Even though I was confident that I held the winning ticket, I told no one about this purchase. I was afraid that the re- action- "You paid one hundred and fifty dollars for a raffle ticket?" did not convey quite the awe that "You bought a brand-new car for one hundred and fifty dollars?" did. I put the ticket in a drawer and told no one.The drawing was set for Friday, the sixteenth of December.

Because of the hectic holiday schedule, my wife and I had made arrangements to drive to my sister's house upstate for the weekend, to celebrate with my family a week early. This would free up Christmas weekend for my grandparents and my in-laws. After work that Friday, I met my wife at her mother's house and told her that I needed to go home to shower and change. She in- formed me that she had brought a change of clothes and that I could shower there. It would have been insane on so many levels to explain that I needed to be home because the church was going to call, - what church? What car? What the hell are you talking about? So, I risked her ire and drove home. Right on schedule, the phone began to ring as I was drying myself off, post shower. Caller ID did not exist on telephones back then, but I knew who was call- ing before I picked up the receiver. It was indeed the church calling to tell me that I had won the car. I still find it difficult to articulate the experience of taking that phone call. And no, it was not the indescribable fact that I had won a car, not just a car but a brand-new Cadillac, but the crazy, otherworldly validation of the positivity I had felt throughout the entire process. Of course, now I had to spill the beans because I needed to claim my winnings. I recruited my sister's husband to drive me to Norwich to pick up the car, and I opted to store it in my mother-in-law's garage until Christmas, now only days away. I told her that I trusted her not to tell anyone about the car because she had had a recent laryngectomy (surgical removal of her voice-box) and she couldn't talk (okay, shame on me, I really did). I backed the car into her garage and hung a huge red ribbon on the front grille, as I had determined from the beginning that my wife would get the car when I won it. The scene was set for Christmas, now only days away.

My wife's family has a tradition of choosing one present to open on Christmas Eve. Generally speaking, my wife would not open anything from me because I would hardly describe my gift-giving as lavish; if she did, she would most likely not have something from me to open on Christmas morning (and exchange days later). So, when I asked her that Christmas Eve if she would like to open her present, she declined. I may have persisted more than usual, and my sister-in-law, noting some urgency in my request, suggested she humor me. Finally, she agreed. When I told her that her present was in the garage, she immediately suspected that I had gotten her a puppy. "It's a puppy," she insisted. "I know you got me a puppy." The entire family walked outside and watched as I opened the garage door. She looked around, going so far as to lean on the hood of her new car, adorned with a giant red ribbon, to peer around in the dark, looking for her puppy. It was her older sister who finally exclaimed that it was a car. "I think he got you a car. Oh my God, I think it's a Cadillac!" I don't know if it was the decorative ribbon or the shiny new vehicle itself that tipped her off, but yes, it was a brand-new car. And even though there was no puppy that Christmas, to this day I remain impressed with the maturity with which my wife handled that disappointment. Whatever happened to the Cadillac, you may wonder? We kept it for a year, and decided to sell it to finance a second child. That's right, we traded in our car for a child and a used station wagon. And pity the child- every time that poor kid misbehaved, I would give my wife "the look" and declare "We should have kept the car."

Wardell Family Archives

If you look closely in the back seat, you cannot see a puppy.

NATIONAL GEOGRAPHIC

My mother was not an Eskimo. I assert that claim because one of my sisters-in-law suspected that she possessed Eskimo DNA (hey, don't ask me), which is why she signed me up for the National Geographic Genome Project. This was not genealogy- National Geographic would not go back fifty generations and tell me which former famous or infamous people I was related to- but would examine my DNA and detail my genetic origins. After swabbing my mouth and sending off the swab for analysis, I received back a report about my mitochondrial (DNA from my mother) sequence, which identifies the branch of the human family tree to which I belong. It's very scientific, but it has something to do with how certain genes or series of proteins mutated over eons. Generally, bragging is difficult for me because that trait had mostly been bred out of my genes, but it turns out that my "clan" (their term, not mine) is Haplogroup W, descended from a woman in the N branch. Hah, top that, other haplogroups! This indicates that my ancestors migrated north from sub-Saharan Africa through the Caucasus in Eastern Europe. To quote from the report, "…your haplogroup is significant because its members constitute one of the four major Ashkenazi Jewish founder lineages." This is not merely significant, it's hugely significant. Understand that my mother's mother (we are talking about DNA passed down on the female side, remember), was born outside of Montreal and was raised, as a number of French-Canadians were, as a Catholic. (As a native French speaker, my grandmother had some peculiar idiomatic malapropisms. My favorite was "Waste not, what not"). Like her three sisters, my mother had been placed in a Catholic boarding school in kindergarten and spent her entire educational life in parochial schools, including a four-year Catholic college. My siblings and I were subjected to the same torture, I mean, afforded the same incredible opportunities, and also spent years in Catholic institutions. (Come to think about it, my career choices may have been informed by my aversion to wearing a jacket and tie, as I had been required to do daily until high school). I thought it ironic, at the very least, to receive this information, and it must have reflected in my countenance when I went to work the next day. My good friend Marian, who is African-American and was adept at reading my emotions, asked me what was on my mind. "I'm conflicted," I allowed. I explained the Genome Project to her and that I had received the results. "That's interesting. So, what's the problem?" she wanted to know. "Well," I explained, "I went home yesterday thinking that I was a white Catholic. It turns out that I'm Black... and Jewish."

SURF AND TURF

I n the '80's I worked as a company driver for a Connecticut wire
mill, which is where I met Curt, and we became good friends. It
wasn't easy to make friends with co-workers as a trucker because,
well, you didn't really "work with" someone in trucking- it was
more like two shifts passing in the night. The wire mill shipped a
lot of its product on flatbed trailers, a type of hauling with which I
had limited exposure, so he stepped forward and mentored me.
Curt taught me the ropes- actually, the chains and binders, as it
were- about securing flatbed loads. He also knew where all of our
customers were located and gave me detailed directions to each,
which went a long way towards mitigating the panic I felt about
driving into New York City. The worst NYC delivery location we
had was on East 18th Street in Manhattan. East 18th Street is a narrow, one-way street where we had to parallel park the truck
against the curb, or risk losing a mirror to a passing garbage truck.
So, not only did I have the anxiety about driving into New York
City, but I had to worry about finding a place to park, and then perform the parallel parking maneuver as well. (This maneuver was
made more difficult because parallel parking involves, as any
driver knows, backing up, which is no easy task at a truck stop; forget about doing it in an articulated vehicle on a narrow street with
early morning commuters and New York city cabs behind you).
The city, to their credit, had imposed a nighttime parking ban on
this street until 6:00 a.m., so we always arrived before that time
and prayed there were no scofflaws out early. One predawn morning, I was about to turn onto 18th Street when I noticed a yellow
police barricade prohibiting all traffic from entering. Naturally, I

did what any native New Yorker would have done, which is get out and move the barrier. As I picked it up and started dragging it out of the way, a young man with a clipboard in his hand ran up to me and asked me what I was doing. "I'm moving the barricade because it's in my way," I answered, even though I thought it was fairly obvious. "The street is closed," he said with great finality. And then, literally, "We're shooting a film." Shooting a film? I wanted to ask him if he was French, because I was under the impression that in New York they "made movies." It turns out that they *were* making a movie- "Bright Lights, Big City," based on a novel by Jay McInerney and starring Michael J. Fox, Phoebe Cates, Kiefer Sutherland and Dianne Wiest- in the penthouse apartment next to my customer's warehouse (You've got to love NY zoning laws). I told the film-shooter with the clipboard that I had 48,000 pounds of steel on the truck and I wasn't going to unload it by hand and carry it down the block. He allowed me to pass, and the movie crew even moved some of their equipment for me so I could roll right into my spot in front of my customer's place of business. To my delight, I noticed that their catering table was fully stocked and unattended, and I had a couple of hours to kill before my customer opened for business.

While we're ranking difficult customer locations, I should mention another nightmare stop, which was in Cambridge, Massachusetts. I had been driving around, lost, and stopped a local driver to ask for directions. He sized up my vehicle and asked me how long my trailer was. I told him forty-five feet, and he said, with certainty, "You can't get in there, you need a forty-footer, max." (Thanks, but don't call me Max). Many of our customers operated their businesses out of old New England mills, in places like Providence, Rhode Island and Worcester, Massachusetts, and we were adept at squeezing our trucks through narrow openings designed a century earlier for much smaller equipment, so I had plenty of confidence that it could be done. I drove to the site and back-and-forthed for nearly an hour, after which I called the dispatcher and told her I could not get into the place without possibly damaging the trailer. She told me to return the load. That night they transferred the freight into a forty-foot trailer and I delivered it the next day, even then with some difficulty. Shortly before I left the wire mill to begin employment with another company, this customer, a Fortune 100 company at the time, finally built a new shipping/receiving dock in the rear of the building which made the delivery immeasurably easier and less stressful.

Still on the subject of nightmare locations? How about a "Philadelphia Story" and a tribute to Frank Rizzo's boys in blue? (Rizzo was the Chief of Police and later the mayor of Philadelphia). I was cruising the streets looking for my destination when I spotted my street ahead on the right. It was, like the aforementioned East 18th Street in New York City, a narrow one-way street with vehicles also parked on both sides, with traffic expected to thread the needle, as it were, between the lines of parked cars. The problem this time was a lovely, expensive Mercedes-Benz parked ass-end out on the right-side of the road; in order to make the turn I had to swing wide to the left to make sure my trailer had enough room to follow. I used the entire road, swinging left all the way to the opposite curb to begin my maneuver, but realized that I still had insufficient room to avoid contact with the offending Mercedes, so I abandoned my truck and tracked down a policeman, beseeching him to have the car towed. His solution- I should complete the turn while he stood near the corner checking my clearance. I didn't need a spotter because I knew the dimensions of my truck and the requisite turning radius so I had my doubts about the efficacy of his plan but he insisted; I was blocking the street and he wanted me out of the way. I got in the truck and began to complete the turn, keeping my eyes on the passenger-side mirror, barely creeping and watching the rear of my trailer inch toward the Benz. I was almost around the corner before my diminishing clearance disappeared completely and my rear tires were flush with the Mercedes. The cop waved me on and yelled "You got it!" so I pulled forward and ripped the left rear quarter-panel off the Mercedes. I put my head in my hands while the policeman walked up to me and said, "That'll teach him. Have a nice day."

Indulge me one more horror story from my tenure at the wire mill. I was back in New York, in Long Island City, searching for the customer's location. I had already stopped for directions and was told to take the last right turn before the Queensboro (59th Street) Bridge. I didn't see the street on my first pass, so I ended up crossing the bridge into Manhattan. I got myself turned around and crossed back and repeated the effort, convinced that I would find it on my second attempt. No such luck- back across the bridge, back into the city. Third time's the charm, I figured, so back to Long Island City and one more approach to the bridge. As far as I could tell, the directions were faulty, or the street simply did not exist, since there was no right turn and I was about to cross the bridge one more time. In a gesture of pure lunacy, I pulled a U-turn in front of the bridge, causing a record-setting, traffic-disrupting, horn-honking, middle-finger waving display that still causes my heart to swell with pride. It turns out, I discovered on my fourth attempt, that there was an unmarked narrow alley that peeled off from the main road just before the bridge entrance. It was not so much a right turn, but a "V"; an off-ramp, more or less, that I found, and took, on my last attempt.

There were many more good days than bad, of course. One day in the late eighties, a truck driver's fantasy came to pass. (No, not that one, pervert). I was eastbound on I-80, heading towards New York City from New Jersey and was maybe thirty-five or forty miles from the George Washington Bridge; traffic was moderate and I anticipated no problem at the bridge tolls. About fifteen minutes later, I realized that the traffic had lightened considerably; even though it was a weekday mid-morning and the commute was over, this was very unusual. About five miles closer to the bridge, I became aware that the road was wide open ahead of me, not a vehicle in sight. I started checking my mirrors and saw empty highway for miles behind me as well. I then checked the sky for traffic helicopters and wondered if perhaps a horrific accident had closed the highway. Had a plane crashed at Teterboro Airport, I wondered? This airport was only a few miles from my current location, close enough to the interstate that an accident could cause panic and traffic disruptions nearby. I passed an exit and saw state police vehicles blocking the ramps and wondered if they were isolating me. Despite some brief paranoia, I ruled this out knowing that I was completely legal; I wasn't overweight, in fact I was deadheading (pulling an empty trailer) back to Connecticut. Something, though, was seriously amiss. I was literally the only vehicle on the highway and had no idea why, so I did what I would do only in the direst of circumstances and turned on AM radio. It took a minute or two to find an all-news station, and another minute or two to discover the reason for my isolation- President Bush (the first one- H.W). was, at that moment on the same Interstate-80 approaching the George Washington Bridge, on his way to address the assembled dignitaries at the United Nations. Somehow, I had managed to avoid the mandate to clear the highway, and had the distinction of leading a presidential motorcade, with the leader of the free world on his way to the U.N. Understand that my fantasy had nothing to do with leading a presidential motorcade, my truck driver's fantasy, shared by hundreds of thousands of motorists daily, was to have the highway all to myself, and to be able to pull into the toll booth at the George Washington Bridge without waiting.

Fast forward a couple of years and I'll attempt to entertain you with another George Washington Bridge story, one with quite a different punchline. I had delivered a truck to a location in southern New Jersey and was riding back to Connecticut with one of our salesmen. It had been an extremely long day for both of us, so when he asked me the best way home, I told him to use the George Washington Bridge. "The GW Bridge? Are you crazy?" "Look," I said, "it'll be midnight by the time we get there. How bad can it be? Plus, it's twenty miles shorter than the Tappan Zee bridge." (These are essentially the only two ways to get to southern New England from New Jersey without crossing into Manhattan though one of the tunnels, and no one in their right mind would consider going into the city a short cut). So, we concurred, the GWB it was. Bad move. Shortly after we passed the turn-off for the longer route north towards the Tappan Zee, we saw brake lights- miles and miles of brake lights. Yes, it was midnight, but we had failed to anticipate the luckless individual whose car had stalled on the bridge. The Port Authority Of New York and New Jersey had a plan for this- tow trucks staged at both ends of the bridge, ready to spring into action to move offending vehicles to restore traffic flow. Unfortunately, this individual (and luckless, as you will see, was an understatement) had gotten out of his stalled vehicle to investigate, was struck by another car and was killed. Tow trucks were useless in these circumstances; a coroner was required. Traffic could not proceed until the man was pronounced dead and removed from the roadway. It took hours to rouse the official and deliver him to the scene; Fred, the salesman, was not pleased. At one point during that very long night he swore he would never take that bridge again, and some hours after that he declared that he was not inclined to solicit my advice in the future, either.

As long as I have ventured light-years away from my original subject (remember Curt?) this incident reminds me of another funny but true story (okay, that last story about the dead guy may not technically qualify as funny, but it *was* absolutely true) that I shared with Fred. He was making a sales call to our dealer in Bangor, Maine, and I was tasked with delivering a new truck to that dealer and then returning with him to Connecticut. I was not aware that he was travelling with a visitor from corporate headquarters in Sweden until he suggested that I meet them both for dinner after I arrived. These corporate visitors came and went frequently; trips to the states were perks offered to a number of the Swedish sales folks, probably for exceeding quotas and things like that. Because I was usually out of town, I became accustomed to seeing strangers with funny accents in the building when I was there and did not give it a second thought. These individuals seemed mostly interested in the generous per diem offered for travel stateside, visits to outlet stores and, with any luck, the purchase of an American muscle car to send home. I pegged Bjorn for one of these as I headed north. I left Connecticut in a snow storm and made it about halfway before the snow turned into a very severe ice storm outside of Boston, inching along with the rest of the traffic until I came to my senses and pulled off the highway seeking shelter. The problem was made more treacherous because I was bobtailing (driving a tractor unit only, with no trailer), which eliminated the risk of a jackknife, but was useless insofar as providing traction. It was clear that I would not make it to Bangor for a free meal on Fred's expense account so I checked into a motel to wait out the storm. I contacted Fred to alert him to my revised schedule, and agreed to meet the two of them for breakfast instead. Since we were to meet very early and I still had a few hours to drive, I went to bed to get some brief sleep. Hours later I was back on the road and was sitting in the restaurant when Fred and Bjorn arrived. I was underwhelmed with our foreign visitor; he seemed like a nice enough fellow but yammered on about the various outlet malls they had visited and the incredible bargains he had found along the way. Definitely not my cup of tea. After breakfast we drove to the dealer, dropped off the truck and headed for home, with Bjorn behind the wheel of his borrowed motor pool car. I climbed into the back seat with the intention of sleeping all the way back to Connecticut, as it had been a harrowing trip and a mostly sleepless night. I had not slept long before we stopped. When I opened my eyes and asked what was going on, Bjorn replied that we had pulled off the turnpike in Freeport because he was going to hit the outlet store at L.L. Bean's, and by the way, since I was awake would I mind finding a place to park the car since there is never convenient parking in a small town like Freeport with a hugely popular tourist attraction like L.L. Bean's? My response is burned into my memory because, as the Fates willed it, it was only after I uttered the immortal refrain "What do I look like, a f**king chauffer?" that I discovered that Bjorn was settling in the states to run the company as the newly installed president. I made Fred, who had given me no heads-up, park the car.

Pardon me, that was some tangent; we'll get back to Bjorn and the Swedes presently. Anyway, Curt was a Mainer, born in Houlton, the last exit on Interstate- 95, on the Canadian border, and he had relocated south with loads of charisma; everyone liked him. I was flattered to be considered a close friend, so, when he moved back to Maine and bought a small general store, I promised to keep in touch. Shortly after he had moved back north, my wife and I were invited to see his new enterprise and to spend some time with him and his new lady friend, so we headed Down East for a memorable couple of days. We hadn't been at the house long, just long enough to set down the suitcases, when he broke the news. "I volunteered you to help out at my club this weekend." "Volunteered how?" I wanted to know. His club had scheduled a fund raiser, like a spaghetti dinner type event, for its members and their guests, and Curt had agreed to prepare this meal for the members. "Great, thanks a lot," I said, not too thrilled at the prospect of spending one of my days off cooking for strangers. "Actually," Curt says, "I offered to cook surf and turf for everyone." "How many is everyone?" I needed to know. The answer- one hundred and twenty-five! - nearly put us back in the car to Connecticut. I was flabbergasted. "You're going to cook lobster and roast beef dinners for one hundred and twenty-five people? You must be out of your mind." "Not me," he insisted. "We are." Did he mean "we are cooking, or "we are out of our minds"? Both, it seems."

The menu, as Curt had promoted it, would also consist of a fish chowder appetizer, then lobster and roast beef and baked potatoes. I don't remember if dessert was on the menu, but if somehow a humongous garbage bag of Pepperidge Farms cookies had magically appeared (stay tuned), we would have found a receptive audience. As I said, Curt was a silver-tongued devil; by the time we had finished our cocktails he had me convinced that we could pull it off. The next morning, we drove to check out the club;

it had a nice industrial-looking kitchen with plenty of stainless-steel counterspace, but still, how in the world could we boil a hundred and twenty-five lobsters on six burners? Particularly since we needed those burners to cook the chowder. And enough roast beef for one hundred and twenty-five people? Impossible, I thought, but Curt had a plan, which commenced at 8:00 in the morning with our first case of beer and lots of potatoes and onions to cut up for the chowder. Curt "knew a guy" with a propane business. Early in the afternoon, a truck arrived- the fuel source for the fifty-five-gallon drums of water that needed to be boiled to cook the lobsters. I felt somewhat better about the situation, but there was a long way to go. A bit later another truck arrived to add more power to the heat. Mr. Charisma had sweet-talked a dozen or so lady friends to start cooking the beef at home, in their own ovens, with an ultimatum to have it at the club in time to serve the guests at five o'clock. I just kept opening beers and chopping onions, thinking that if things went south, so what? I would never see these people again. Things were fairly placid until the guests sat down and it was time to serve. Fortunately, Curt had also recruited a significant number of his fans as wait staff, and they did a fantastic job of getting dinners to everyone in a timely manner. Despite the logistics of preparing and serving one hundred and twenty-five meals, we actually pulled it off. When it was over, Curt's fellow club members demanded a curtain call, and we were rewarded with a standing ovation as we emerged from the kitchen. I must say that single gesture was a fantastic token of approval for my initial effort as a sous chef. I found it nearly as satisfying as the seven lobster tails I devoured for the effort.

THE SWEDISH CONNECTION

I had a friend from college and she, like a number of my very conventional contemporaries, could not understand what appeal trucking had for me. She always thought it was a passing fancy ("Passing Fancy," as it happens, was my CB handle) and that I would grow out of it. "Sure," she'd argue, "But what are you going to do when you're forty?" It amuses me to think that at one point we were so naïve as to consider forty too hold to have a job like that. "I'll cross that bridge when I get to it" I assured her, with a driving metaphor. Crossing a bridge may be a metaphor for committing to a decision, but, in the real world, bridges are sometimes best not crossed. The first bridge that I remember collapsing was the "Silver Bridge" spanning the Ohio River from Gallipolis, Ohio, to Point Pleasant, West Virginia which collapsed on December 15, 1967. I remember this bridge because it was just down-river from where I would be crossing the Ohio a few days hence as I made my way home from college for Christmas break. A theory put forth by my Physics professor was that the harmonics created by idling car and truck motors caused the bridge to vibrate to the point of collapse. (Wait: A theory is a hypothesis that has been proven, so this must have been a hypothesis). Whatever we call it, let's just say that it resonated. Fear of crossing bridges is a relatively common phobia called "gephyrophobia," and most truck drivers have probably had a gephyr or two at some point in their travels. On June 29, 1983, a 100-foot section of Interstate 95 collapsed into the Mianus River in Connecticut, mere hours before I was scheduled to drive across it, taking cars and trucks with it, and forcing traffic in both directions to detour through the very wealthy town of Greenwich, causing locals to be late to any of their eight country clubs for six months, until the bridge was replaced and reopened. And, one of the more recent, generating the most media coverage by far, was the I-35 bridge in Minneapolis, which collapsed on August 1, 2007. If you ever drove a vehicle that weighed forty tons and you didn't worry about the condition of the bridges from time to time, I envy you. (More on bridge limits later). And, sure enough, when I was forty years old, an opportunity fell in my lap that changed the trajectory of my career.

When my son became school buddies with a young British lad, the mothers were encouraged to meet in order to arrange play dates. As a consequence, the mothers became good friends and the next step, evidently, was to get the fathers involved. I wanted no part of this, for the simple reason that I disdained entertaining and didn't like meeting strangers. My wife assured me that he was very interesting and was "involved in trucking." A date was set and the evening went extremely well. They were a charming and funny couple and it turns out my wife had accurately portrayed the husband- he *was* very interesting and he was involved in trucking. His involvement was on a somewhat different plane than mine, however. He had been recruited by Scania, a Swedish truck manufacturer whose interests he represented in Great Britain, to help build the brand in the United States as the Vice-President of Marketing. This was essentially a U.S. start-up company with about fifty employees, although, at the time, the brand internationally was the fourth largest truck manufacturer in the world! And you've never heard of it, am I right? The company faced a couple of enormous obstacles. The first, and the one that proved fatal to their American expansion plans, was their business model, wildly successful on other continents, of building a franchise network one dealer at a time. Whereas Volvo, another Swedish truck company, had bought the assets of Ford when they shuttered their truck business, Scania was attempting to sell trucks without a nationwide network to provide parts and service. It turns out this was a bad move. The second, more immediate problem, was that Swedish designers had imagined that American streets were paved with gold, or, at the very least, incredibly smooth bitumen, and sorely underestimated the stress these trucks would undergo operating on some of the most miserable roads in the northeast. As a result of this error, compounded with their effort to save weight, they had under-engineered one of their suspension options offered on their trucks sold in the United States. Scania trucks were hauling freight across Europe, Asia, Australia and South America, but trucks sold in America were routinely operating on third-world roads like the Long Island Expressway (LIE), the Brooklyn-Queens Expressway (BQE) and the Cross-Bronx Expressway in New York City and began showing premature signs of wear, so the Swedes prepared a campaign to upgrade every truck so outfitted with a "new, improved" suspension. The decision had been made to ship all new suspension parts to corporate headquarters in Connecticut and the retrofits would be done "in house" by a team of mechanics dedicated to this project. Having made this determination, they needed to hire a driver to pick up all of the two hundred and twenty affected trucks and bring them into the shop in Connecticut. This is where I arrived on the scene. But first...

THE TRAVELING TRUCK SHOW

I n 1989 Scania was named "Truck of the Year" in Europe, and the corporate board in Sweden had planned a huge promotion to introduce the new models in America. This involved a military-style campaign of vehicles and equipment to be trucked across eight states over six weeks where the new models would be showcased at truck shows and extant Scania dealers. This "Traveling Truck Show," as it was billed, consisted of about twenty trailer trucks hauling tents, lights, generators, marketing materials, cutaway displays of engines and transmissions, a Scania race truck and a Saab dragster, a number of assorted show trucks in various configurations such as a dump truck and a garbage truck, an antique Scania beer truck, two Saab cars which had recently set endurance records at Talladega race track (Saab's 1986 media information explains: "The cars were driven constantly at about 220 KPH [136.7 MPH], but the pit stops reduced the average speed to between 210 [130.5] and 215 KPH [133.6 MPH]. Each car covered a distance of 5,000 kilometers [3,107 miles] a day–which corresponds to driving from Sweden's capital, Stockholm, to Rome and back) and a rotating assortment of Saab company cars driven by various sales, service and parts personnel traveling in support of the event. (Scania was the truck and bus division of Saab-Scania, hence the preponderance of Saab cars). My principal campaign duty was to meet with those truck owners whose vehicles were included in the pending suspension upgrade and to outline our upcoming program to them. (At my disposal would be a small fleet of loaner vehicles for their use while their trucks were in our shop; these could be offered to allay any fears of lost revenue and to introduce them to the new models). At some point during this promotional caravan my boss was recalled and left for home in the United Kingdom. In a brief ceremonial transfer over cocktails in a hotel bar, I was handed a large three-ring binder containing all the information I would need for the suspension changeover and was told "Good luck." By virtue of this brief exchange, and the timeless virtue of being in the right place at the right time, I had graduated from being one more driver for the caravan to the Project Coordinator for a multi-million-dollar service initiative.

One of the highlights of the truck world on the East Coast every Spring is an event called "The Diesel Nationals", held at Raceway Park in Englishtown, New Jersey. As I described it to friends, it was "Woodstock for Truckers." Like Woodstock, the crowd arrived early, days before the three-day event started. Like Woodstock, the crowd shared a passion- not music, but their trucks and the trucking culture. And, like Woodstock, the crowd shared "a look"- not so much the long hair and bell-bottoms of twenty years earlier, but trucker hats, beer guts and tattoos (this was before every Tom, Dick and barista was sporting "arm-sleeves" and full body tats). The stage was not a platform for the various bands scheduled to perform, but a drag strip where trucks would battle for performance supremacy in quarter-mile increments over the next three days. And, as part of "The Traveling Truck Show" introductory campaign, Scania sponsored the event. As such, we had access to the track tower where a stocked buffet table entertained guests throughout the three-day event. After the races concluded on Sunday, after winners in each class were determined, and, after prizes were awarded, we packed up and headed to the next show. The penultimate event of the truck caravan was Indianapolis, Indiana, where we had one more show before we turned around and headed back east for a final show in Syracuse, New York. Our schedule put us in conflict with Race Week in Indianapolis, and, since all of the hotel space there had been reserved by the Indianapolis 500 crowd, we laid over in Richmond, Indiana for the weekend. By this point a number of us had been on the road for a month without a break, so management suggested an "all-hands" Happy Hour in the hotel bar before giving us the long Memorial Day weekend off.

Let me acknowledge here the incredible drinking prowess of the Swedish natives. As one of my colleagues from northern Sweden put it, "Chris, Swedes drink all the time. In the north, where I am from, it stays light all night in the summer, so when you walk out of the bar it is still light and no one goes home. During the winter, it gets dark at two o'clock in the afternoon. It is so depressing that everyone goes to bars after work and drinks all night." Forewarned is forearmed, they say. We met in the bar and proceeded to order rounds of drinks. Many, many rounds. One of the Sales Managers kicked it off. He was a scotch drinker and ordered a round for the room, they were delivered to the tables and duly drunk. The Service Manager was a beer guy; he ordered a round, and we chased the scotch with beer. There were martini drinkers and rum enthusiasts and we continued apace. After mixing copious amounts of many mixed drinks, one of the Swedes ordered "caffe kas" for the room. That stopped us in our tracks. Not familiar with "caffe kas"? Nor were most of us, but the Swedes seemed delighted and, by this point in the proceedings, the rest of us were in no position to argue. We watched in fascination as shot glasses were dispensed to the tables and a penny was placed in each. The bar staff then poured coffee into our shots until the penny disappeared in the dark liquid in the bottom of the glass. The piece de resistance was the vodka, poured in sufficient volume to dilute the coffee until the penny was again visible at the bottom of the glass. Many shots of this cocktail were consumed to various toasts in two increasingly incoherent languages. Vodka-flavored coffee- yummy! I guess if one is going to be completely out of his mind drunk, he'd want enough caffeine in his system to prevent him from sleeping it off. Most of the rest of the evening is forever lost in an alcohol-induced fog, but I do remember well a number of the Swedes picking up the piano and carrying it out of the bar and into the hotel lobby. The offense? The flustered piano player could not honor repeated shouted requests to play the Swedish National Anthem, even with the entire chorus of Swedes assisting him with the melody a cappella. Days later, I asked the boss why hotel management hadn't thrown us out and he said we were ordering drinks faster than they could make them, and the bar bill was sufficiently large enough to indemnify us for any damage that might have occurred. We were loud, no doubt, but, with the exception of the piano incident, pretty well-behaved. And, in addition to the enormous bar tally, tips dispensed to the wait staff and the aggrieved piano player who performed his last set in the lobby adequately compensated all concerned for any inconvenience incurred.

TRUCK SCALES

Y ou've all seen weigh stations, no? These are placed at intervals along the highways to ensure that trucks are obeying the legal limits that they are allowed to carry. My intention is not to bore the reader with esoterica about weight laws, but to describe a funny but true event that occurred on our return from Indianapolis. Truck scales do not just determine gross vehicle weights (total weight of the truck and its contents), but axle weights, which are configured by what's called the bridge formula. Think of it this way- a bridge is engineered to sustain a certain amount of weight. If a truck is seventy feet long, that gross weight needs to be spread out over the entire length of the vehicle so as not to exceed the design limit of the bridge. An eighteen-wheeled tractor and trailer combination has five axles, so the total vehicle weight must be apportioned equally (more or less) over each axle. Got it? Great, because as we were heading back east, I was pulling the trailer loaded with giant concrete blocks. Giant concrete blocks, you ask? Yes, these blocks were used to support, via guy wires, the massive light towers that we set up at every show location to light up the grounds around our display tents, since our displays were open until late in the evening. However, these blocks were very heavy and put too much weight on my drive axles (the rear tires on the tractor, just under the trailer hitch, as opposed to the front, or steering axle) so I was instructed to pull around behind the scales and bring my paperwork into the weigh station. The rest of the caravan, not understanding what was going on, followed me around back and parked alongside me. As comical a scene as this created, it turned out that it was my good fortune that they had followed me, since I would need to unload the forklift from another trailer to reposition my load. The next hour was a text-book display of synergy, as we had conducted these maneuvers repeatedly for the last month. I unchained my load as the forklift was unloaded from its trailer and positioned next to mine. The blocks were moved and re-secured as the forklift was reloaded. I pulled back around to the scale, was given a thumbs-up and we were off. It was a beautiful thing to behold, if synergy is your thing.

On a subsequent trip, I had been driving for a couple of hours on a cold, snowy day before encountering the first open scales. Because it was so cold nothing was melting, instead, most of the messy stuff had been kicked up and was collecting beneath the trailer and refreezing near the rear wheels. Thus, I was not sur-prised to be directed around back and invited in to chat with the Highway Patrol. They suggested that I knock some of the ice off from under the trailer and get re-weighed. The problem was, all I had was a regular claw hammer in my tool kit, and a job this size required a big sledge hammer, like the one the guy parked next to me was using. Truck drivers are usually are pretty amenable to helping their fellow truckers, but this old boy was having none of it. "Get your own damn sledge hammer," he advised. "Thanks for your help, asshole," was my immediate and clever riposte. I had sliding tandems on my trailer (these are adjustable wheels which can be moved forward or backward to accommodate differ-ent overall length limits in various states, but may also be used to reposition the weight distribution without having to move the freight itself). If I could slide the tandems back before I pulled on the scale, you see, the total weight of the ice would be spread out over a greater distance and just might make me legal. The problem was, even in the best conditions this can be a difficult maneuver, as road grit and rust develop under the trailer and in the sliding mechanism itself to prevent the axles from sliding easily on the frame. I didn't have a Plan B so I gave it a shot. First try- no (d)ice, everything was frozen solid. I tried it again, giving it as much power as I dared and released the clutch. Again nothing. But wait. The torqueing of the tractor back against the trailer was enough to loosen the ice and a ton of it crashed down onto the pavement. The wheels had not moved, but the physics were similar to twisting a plastic ice cube tray to free the frozen cubes. With that, I released the trailer brake, put the truck in gear and wished my compatriot good luck with the sledge hammer, although I may have Freudian-slipped on the ice a bit as it came out sounding more like "Stick it up your ass, loser," before rolling back on the scale.

One more funny but true story about truck scales, this time at a weigh station in Ohio. Again, I was instructed to pull around back and bring in my paperwork. The problem this time was not my weight, but my fuel sticker. You may be learning more about trucks than you ever cared to, but trucks in interstate transportation are required to pay a road use tax for every mile that is driven in each state and must display fuel permits to indicate they have sought permission to use these roads. Let's say a particular state has a ten-cent road tax added to its cost of diesel fuel. My truck averaged eight miles per gallon. If I drove eight hundred miles in that state, I would burn one hundred gallons of fuel and owe the state one hundred times the fuel tax on that fuel, or ten dollars. In lieu of making a payment by mail, a driver could purchase enough fuel in that state to offset this tax. These tax forms must be filled out every month, accounting for every mile for every state in which that truck has driven and, it became my responsibility to file these monthly taxes. The bottom line is that trucks were prohibited from operating in any state for which the truck did not have a fuel permit. Hence, the instruction for me to pull around back.

I did have a fuel permit decal for Ohio, though. The problem was that it was not visible to the scale operator because it had been mistakenly affixed to the driver's side of the truck, rather than the passenger's side as required in Ohio. I tried some fast talking and explained to the scale operator that technically it *was* on the passenger side, since Scanias were Swedish trucks and Swedes, like the British, drove on the right-hand side of the road; this configuration made our driver side their passenger side. I was not telling an outright lie when I made this assertion because Swedes did, indeed, drive on the opposite side- until 6:00 in the morning on September 3, 1967, or, as it was called, Högertrafikomläggningen (Right-Hand Traffic Diversion) Day, or Dagen H, for short. Every single street sign in the country had literally been switched over to the opposite side overnight. It was pretty much beside the point, however, since the scale operator, a bored bureaucrat who had probably been watching trucks roll by for hours, merely shrugged his shoulders and let me go.

HAPPY HOUR

*A priest, a minister and a rabbi walk into a bar. The bartender,
washing glasses, looks up and says, "What is this? A joke?"*

Orange, Connecticut, the corporate home of Scania USA, was a
reasonably tolerable commute for employees who lived east
of New Haven, except on Friday afternoons during the summer.
The commute became intolerable as thousands of beach-going
vacationers left work early for campsites along the coast or for
through passage to Cape Cod and the Islands (Block Island, Mar-
tha's Vineyard, Nantucket, et. al) and were forced to navigate the
three-lane Quinnipiac River Bridge at the junction of interstates
I-91 and I-95. That's right, two interstate highways converged into
a single passage east onto a three-lane bridge that narrowed to two
lanes when the bridge reached the east side of the river. It was hellish. (Years earlier, I had left Los Angeles after midnight and was
heading east. The interstate highway I was on was at least four
lanes in each direction, maybe five. There was absolutely no traffic
and I positioned the truck somewhere in the middle to allow myself a cushion in case I drifted a bit. I got pulled over- I was not
speeding, there was no other traffic on the road and it was two
o'clock in the morning. The cop suggested that I knew why I had
been pulled over. I replied that I had no idea. "You were driving in
the restricted lane." "Restricted lane?" I questioned. "Yes, trucks
are restricted from the left two lanes (I don't remember exactly
how many restricted lanes there were on this humongous highway). Don't you have that law in... (looks down at my license) Connecticut?" I had to laugh. "Sir, Interstate 95, which we call the Connecticut Turnpike is 112 miles across from New York to Rhode Island and it's only two lanes most of its length. I've never been on a

road this big before." He let me go with a chuckle and a verbal warning). Anyway, to avoid this hellish commute, it was our habit to meet for drinks after work on Fridays and wait until traffic subsided. Most bars back then served food during Happy Hour so we could eat, drink and be merry. The problem, as I earlier indicated, was that there was no word in the Swedish vocabulary for moderation. Thus, after a long week of trying to keep our fledgling enterprise afloat, Happy Hour often stretched into Happy Hours. One such Friday afternoon, a number of us found ourselves at a Mexican restaurant notable for its generous and excellent margaritas. I knew better. I refrained from tequila, but confess to a Dos Equis or two. As you entered the restaurant, there was a small maître d' station by the door; the bar was immediately to the right and the restaurant tables were off to the left. At some point during the evening, we heard sirens, emergency lights flooded the front windows and an ambulance crew rushed into the restaurant. A diner had choked on his burrito, EMTs arrived, performed the Heimlich maneuver and departed. Since I was seated on the bar stool nearest the front door, I took advantage of the excitement and the absence of staff and began greeting the diners myself as they entered. "Do you prefer choking or non-choking?" I would ask, as they entered the restaurant. My drinking companions were having a good laugh, but the staff did not share our sense of humor and escorted me out. My friends delighted in that, as well, but I got the last laugh- they had to reckon with my unpaid bar tab.

I did not exaggerate when I discussed the drinking stamina of my Swedish colleagues. I cannot remember a single company occasion where alcohol was not available. Once, when a high-level dignitary was visiting from corporate headquarters in Sweden, we were summoned to a breakfast meeting at his hotel for an update on our financial condition. I was seated at his table with some folks from the sales department, when one of them said sycophantically, "You speak English so well. Since we represent a Swedish corporation, shouldn't we all be required to learn to speak Swedish?" Why wouldn't they be fluent? After all, English is taught in Swedish schools starting in the first grade. I would have been fluent if Rose Murray had been teaching me Swedish instead of scheduling meetings with my parents to discuss my behavior. Also, our corporate name was Scania **USA**, so I was miffed at the transparency of this ass-kissing gesture. In my inimitable way, I informed the assembled guests that, although I couldn't speak for the rest of the Yanks at the table, I could speak a little Swedish. As they turned and looked at me, I raised my Bloody Mary and said "Absolut." Okay, maybe the only Swedish I knew was the brand-name of a Swedish vodka, but it sure took the wind out of that gubbslem's sails. (Loosely translated- something like geezer phlegm, a popular Swedish expression for what is otherwise known as the old-boy's network).

Another time three of us had gone out to lunch (no Swedes, no drinking), and we chose a submarine sandwich shop near work. I consider myself tallish at 6'3" but that day I was the shortest banana in the bunch. My coworkers were 6'4" and 6'7" and we waited in line in that ascending order. As it happened, we were all wearing branded shirts bearing the company name. The employee taking our orders was not particularly tall; it would be a stretch to say he was medium height. To use a sub shop analogy, he was the six-inch sub to our foot-long sandwiches. After he took the three orders, he looked up at us and said, "Let me ask you guys. Is there a height requirement where you work?" This is no tall tale but a short story, another funny thing that was true because his curiosity seemed genuine, and the question was asked, it appeared, in all sincerity.

TOO MUCH OF A GOOD THING

N aturally, it was too good to be true. My Swedish employer sold its Saab car division to General Motors in 1990 and GM immediately announced plans to move Saab's headquarters to Atlanta. The truck division, already on shaky ground financially (it actually lost money every time it sold a truck. The US entered a short recession in 1990, which, while it only lasted only eight months through March 1991, was long enough to apply a knockout blow to Scania USA. Truck sales had been depressed nationally for a while; the unfavorable exchange rate between the Swedish kronor and the American dollar merely exacerbated the problem) could not sustain itself without the deeper pockets of its money-making corporate partner so the decision was made to "pull the plug" and abandon its effort to sell trucks in the states. I would be retained until the suspension project was completed, but it was clearly crossroads time. I was approaching that age where I should have been buying an impractical red sports car, but since I was on the cusp of losing my job, I couldn't really embrace the idea; besides, I never pictured myself as a cliché. In a manner of speaking, I had never left trucking; I was still in a truck and on the road more days than I was in the office, but I had to confront the implications of returning to hauling freight again. The perks of corporate life- a company credit card, eating in real restaurants and sleeping in nice hotels had spoiled me for the rigors of life lived on the road. My former employer at the wire mill would welcome me back, but returning would entail starting back at the bottom of the seniority list. That would mean handling the loads that no one else wanted with daily trips to New York City, Long Island and northern New Jersey. Ugh. So, I looked around and found temporary work driving for Pepperidge Farms, which was a division of Campbell Soup, thinking that I might be able to leverage this into full-time work hauling soup over the road. This plan failed to materialize, but I did enjoy that brief period of transition. The people there were excellent to work for and they had generous employee discounts on their products, one of which played a role in an unusual funny but true situation I am about to relate. To set the scene: on this particular trip I was hauling a load of vanilla wafers to the chocolatier so the secret ingredient (chocolate) in these Pepperidge Farms Cookies could be added between the wafers and subsequently packaged as Milanos. For those of you unfamiliar with Pepperidge Farms Milano cookies, they are a treat, an addictive treat for me at least, suggested by an Italian pastry. A few days later the cookies were ready and I was dispatched back to the chocolatier to pick up the finished product. When the truck was loaded, I pulled away from the dock, closed the doors, secured and sealed the trailer, and went to the shipping office to sign and collect the paperwork. As I attended to these details the shipper pointed to a giant plastic garbage bag and asked what I wished to do with it. "What is it?" I asked. "Seconds," was the reply. These were the cookies that failed to make the varsity; chipped or broken perhaps, or they had excess chocolate dripping down the outside of the wafer which supposedly made them unappetizing. I would have put them in the trailer, but the seal was in place and a driver does not remove a seal under any circumstances, so I took the bag with me, threw it in the cab and left for home. I had driven for a couple of hours when the hunger pangs started. I was still some distance from a truck stop so, naturally, I dipped into the garbage bag for a cookie or two to sustain me. If you've ever snacked on peanuts, popcorn or potato chips and finished the entire bag you may relate to my dilemma. The problem was, this sixty-five-gallon garbage bag held more cookies than I could tolerate and I had no self-control so I partook in an orgy of overeating that approached grotesquerie. I would swear off the cookies until the sugar rush subsided and then eat "just one more." I battled admirably for a hundred miles or so, until compelled to either throw them away or throw them up. "They fell off the back of the truck," I anticipated my answer when I returned to the warehouse. Despite my best effort, I failed to make a dent in that bag, so, I tossed them into a trash container at the next rest area. With no "sell-by" date on the garbage bag, "dumpster-divers" reclaiming that bag would have themselves a life-time supply. The question of this bag of seconds did not come up on my return to Connecticut.

MID-LIFE CRISIS

I t is possible the reader is familiar with the aphorism "Truck drivers know the best places to eat." Wrong. Truck drivers know where the biggest parking lots are. In the old days, it is true that truckers did find places where the service was timely, the food was decent, the prices were reasonable, and refills on coffee were free, but that was before the interstate road system was developed. The interstate system was initiated by Dwight Eisenhower, who had been elected president in 1952, mostly by virtue of his military service as the Supreme Commander of Allied forces in Europe during World War II. He had returned deeply impressed with the roads in Europe, particularly the German Autobahn, because he understood the military significance that roads like these had for the German Blitzkrieg- moving massive quantities of war materiel quickly. So, like the internet and Global Positioning Satellites (GPS), the Interstate road system was first conceived as a military application.

Open a road atlas of the United States and look at the interstates (major highways that are indicated with an "I" designation). The easiest way to describe the system is to say that it is a grid of limited-access roads running north and south identified by odd numbers, and east and west identified by even numbers. The route numbers increase in value as you move east (I-5 runs the entire length of the west coast, I-95 runs the length of the opposite coast) and north, (Interstate 10 runs along the southern United States from Jacksonville, Florida to Los Angeles, while I-90 traverses from Boston to Seattle). New roads get built based on metrics like population growth, traffic density and political clout; these tend to be designated with a prefix (2,4,6 and 8 are typically circumferential highways- highways that move traffic around, rather than through a city center- and odd-numbered prefixes that tend to be spur roads which deviate from the main road to deliver traffic to a city center, for example, or to connect two or more interstates). One last lesson about interstate nomenclature- have you ever found yourself on the wrong side of the highway as your exit approaches? You can avoid crossing speeding lanes of traffic by looking carefully at the exit sign next time you approach- the position of the exit number on the sign will tell you which side of the road your exit will be on. Is the number bolted on the top left of the exit sign? Move to the left lane because that's the side of the road the exit lane will be on. No more panic moves at sixty miles per hour.

In spite of being a "roads scholar," the Pepperidge Farms situation did not become permanent and the depressed economy made our decision for us: we would sell our house, pack our things and move. This may seem drastic but it wasn't as impulsive as it sounds; my brother had remained in North Carolina after college and frequent visits south had convinced us that it was a likely eventual destination. My parents had already made the move to coastal Carolina from Connecticut after retirement; the climate beckoned. As I explained to my wife, if I had to start at the bottom again, I'd prefer to do it where the roads were better and there was less traffic, in a more temperate environment with better weather and less snow. If you had ever worked a mile in my shoes (atop a loaded flatbed trying to unfold a frozen tarpaulin when the temperature was in single digits) you would understand my motivation to relocate to warmer climes.

Despite the presence of previously relocated relatives, it was still daunting for my two young children and a wife who was having second thoughts about leaving her family and friends behind. Call me old-fashioned, but I still pictured myself as a role model and I didn't want my children to see their unemployed father hanging around the house as they went off to school. I needed to find a job. I was told that the best way to "get one's foot in the door" at Duke University was through their Temporary Services Office. I did get my foot in the door- little pay and no benefits, but it was a very big door (between the University and the Medical Center they employ 25,000 people). Temporary help at Duke were not well-compensated; I would be exchanging my Connecticut unemployment benefit for a smaller paycheck, but I was heading to work every morning and I was convinced that our future was bright. The temporary job did indeed lead to a permanent, full-time position, where I managed to survive for sixteen additional years. By the end of those sixteen years I was more than ready to move on; it was a bad news/good news situation that delivered me. The mortgage-inflicted housing debacle and subsequent economic meltdown of 2008 had hit the Duke endowment particularly hard- the fund had lost a third of its value, forcing Duke to examine staffing and payroll requirements. This led them to offer retirement-inducement packages to a select subset of employees. Duke had a "Rule of Seventy-five" whereby employees whose age and years of service totaled seventy-five could retire with a pension and health benefits. To qualify more people, Duke would sweeten the deal by adding an additional five years of service to each employee, thereby increasing the eligibility pool. Intimations had been made that Duke would eliminate a number of positions if staff did not retire in sufficient numbers and I had annoyed enough people to feel vulnerable. Besides, since I had already achieved the magic number of seventy-five, the five-year enhancement to my pension made staying impractical.

NEXT STOP: PUBLIC SERVICE

I mentioned earlier the cross-country road trip that I did with my son, post-retirement. I recall also mentioning that I returned to trucking after I retired. These two events were not entirely unrelated, as the first (the cross-country road trip) renewed my vigor for getting back on the road. Consequently, not long after my road trip with Travis, I found myself in a truck one morning driving east from Dallas; the previous night Mother Nature had produced an epic winter storm that had covered the southeast in ice. My co-driver was in the sleeper berth, and I was inching along in a traffic jam that extended from Texas to Tennessee- the entirety of our route to our delivery location- the massive FedEx hub in Memphis. (If FedEx and UPS merged, would the new corporate entity be called Fed-UP?) I believe I may have covered twenty miles in the four or five hours he slept. Eventually, he awoke and sat down in the passenger seat next to me. He looked at the weather, he looked at the traffic, he looked at me. You could not imagine worse conditions to be driving a truck. "What are you smiling at?" he asked me. "I was just thinking how much better this is than my last job." How bad was the weather? We made it to the next exit before being directed off the exit ramp- they had shut down the interstate. How much did I hate my previous job? Re-read this paragraph.

I only made it six months behind the wheel this time before calling it quits, largely due to my lack of time at home. In those six months I got home twice; three days each for Thanksgiving and Christmas, and my wife complained that this was not how she pictured living out our "Golden Years." I concurred. Plus, I had managed to pick the worst months of the year to drive seven thousand miles a week back and forth across the country- October to March, or, as it is called in most parts of the United States, winter. Add to that a nervous co-driver with eight months experience (heck, I was the one who should have been nervous) who questioned my abilities and the decision to re-retire was easy. His doubts became manifest during a snow storm in Colorado when an on-coming truck flashed his high-beams; this is generally interpreted as a cautionary signal to slow down. Instead of using my brakes I eased off the accelerator and began to gear down, allowing the engine to slow the truck rather than the brakes. As I went around the curve, I saw the problem- vehicles everywhere- across the road, in the median and on the shoulder. Although one's impulse is to hit the brakes when confronted with this scenario, I understood it was precisely that impulse that had created this mess, so I continued to gear down and steer around and through the wreckage. One method sure to induce a skid on ice is to lock up your wheels; the wheels must keep rolling to reduce the risk of skidding. Emerging unscathed and still upright on the other side, my co-driver remarked, "You were going kind of fast." Too fast, I thought. Some people are really hard to please; he was probably annoyed that I had not hit the brakes. The situation was reversed when he took over. I climbed into the sleeper berth and immediately fell asleep. A short time later he woke me up to tell me that the "Chains Required" signs were flashing. Operating your truck without tire chains at this point was foolhardy, and costly if you were pulled over and cited. "What do you want to do?" he asked. Right, now he was seeking my counsel. Giving him the benefit of my twenty years of experience, I told him what I wanted to do was to go back to sleep, but, I added, he should forget the chains for now and get some sleep as well. Drivers can't make very good time with chains on their tires, they take (uncompensated) time to put on and take off, and they tend to wreak havoc with the rubber. I always found that it was better to grab some sleep and wait for the weather to change, unless you drive in a place like Alta, Utah, where their annual total of 583 inches would suggest hibernation as the preferable option.

Duke was an exponentially more difficult environment to navigate, believe it or not, than driving a truck on slick roads. In the first place, the overriding management principle I heard most often was "...because we've always done it that way, that's why." Big sigh. Really? Emerging unscathed and still upright on the far side of a ten-car pile-up was a seasonal hazard for truck drivers; independent thinking- a critical need for life on the road- was not valued at Duke. Duke, bifurcated as it was between the University and the Medical Center, created a duopoly of competing agendas. In addition to this, both institutions had their own scores of departments, each with individual self-interests and their own vehicles to administer, all of which required me to interact with multiple sets of management. This arrangement also explained the vast numbers of "task forces" assigned to the issue of problem-solving. No one wanted to upset their sinecure so these task forces provided anonymous cover for unpopular decisions. I frequently rendered unpopular decisions with the knowledge they would be unpopular but most safety issues could not wait for the convention of a task force to mull things over. It fascinated me that people I met outside of the institution were envious when I told them where I worked. The "Gothic Wonderland" was indeed a beautiful campus; its architecture most inspiring. The university had an excellent academic reputation and the Medical Center provided ground-breaking and award-winning care. Duke even had a pretty good basketball team, but these attractions did not translate to job satisfaction, and sclerotic management where every manager protected her own fiefdom and where little guidance and no support were offered led to great frustration. That frustration boiled over on September 11, 2001. I was standing at the bus stop in front of the University Chapel with one of my ex-bosses when word started to spread about the attack on the World Trade Center. I was aware that he, too, was feeling enormously frustrated since he had recently been "down-sized" with a vague title and a small office in the basement of the student center. The two of us adjourned to the Student Union where we found the nearest television set and watched in disbelief as the first building collapsed. I turned to him and said, "I knew there had to be worse places to work than Duke." Too soon? Of course. Said reflexively without thinking, my glib remark was obviously impulsive and ill-considered and, given the enormity of what we had just witnessed, it would have been prudent to hold my tongue. I had developed the habit of saying what I was thinking early on; one look at that Permanent Record would tell you all you need to know. (Believe me, I'm well aware that this habit reappears from time to time in my narrative. A good friend once observed that the only time I opened my mouth was to change feet, an astute and clever observation, for sure. However, I would be remiss if I failed to include an even better line he delivered, a beauty he uttered while riding in an increasingly warm and stuffy truck. When requested to open his window he declined, explaining with this quick and simple excuse- "I forgot my coif medicine."

You might ask, why did I persist in that environment? Great question, if so asked. Let's face it, job fulfillment comes in many flavors, not least among them is a steady paycheck. But mine derived, at that time, from the Tuition Benefit Plan offered to University employees. I had one son in college and, in 2001, when the World Trade Center was attacked, I still had one in high school; the plan covered eight semesters of tuition for each of two children. I did not intend to leave before exhausting that benefit. Once my second son had graduated, there was little incentive to stay, and the retirement inducement was simply icing on the cake. But no job is completely negative. One of the few routines that I did enjoy was the annual "Bus Roadeo." To the uninitiated, a bus roadeo is a test of skills requiring bus drivers to navigate their vehicles through a course of backing and turning exercises while being timed. The course is laid out with cones and barrels and striking these result in point assessments. Like golf, low score wins.

These roadeos occur on local levels, initially, with the winners moving to regional, state and national competitions. Roadeos are great for team-building and they provide annual bragging rights, both within an organization and between agencies. To prepare for our participation, we had set up a course in one of the massive Medical Center parking lots which was mostly vacant on the weekends. My boss arrived to observe and, during the practice, she told me she wanted to drive the course. She had never driven a bus and she was not properly licensed, nor medically qualified, but we were on private property, so I set her up behind the wheel. Of course, she ran over every cone. When she was done, she declared that it had been loads of fun and she wanted me to teach her how to drive and to train her to get her Commercial Drivers' License. I told her that we should do it as soon as possible, and she asked me why. "Because you've been here two years, so you're about to be replaced." Although my straight speaking was a constant irritant to her, my assessment was spot-on and she was gone within six months, absent a Commercial Driver's License, I should add. I am honest enough to admit that driving a truck for twenty years may have reinforced my native iconoclasm regarding business best practices, so the six directors who swore I was impossible to work with clearly knew what they were talking about. I outlasted all six of them.

Wardell Family Archives

Souvenir T-shirt from the 2007 North Carolina Public Transportation Roadeo

In addition to esprit de corps, these roadeos provided opportunities to network with other industry professionals. Therefore, I was not completely astonished when I received a call out of the blue about a job opening from the city transit provider-Durham Area Transit Authority, hereinafter referred to as DATA. Hearing that I had retired from Duke, they were interested in interviewing me for an operations position. I submitted to the interview and was hired. I believe the line that secured the position was that working for local transit was an opportunity to "give back to the community." Typing this line, I realize it sounds trite, like some self-serving response one might offer at a job interview, but after working in the rarified air that was Duke, working with the public seemed like a really terrific soul-cleansing opportunity.

A SOCIOLOGY LESSON

As I anticipated, there could not have been starker cultural differences between the demographics of the typical Duke bus rider and the population of passengers who rode the city bus. The students who rode the bus at the university (anticipate some stereotyping here) were mostly white and many were raised in privileged circumstances. (One day, I was asked to drive some outside contractors to the football stadium where they were headed to meet their work crews. As I swiped my card to enter the gated parking lot, one of them mentioned how well the professors must be paid, given the preponderance of expensive European cars and high-dollar SUVs. "This is a student parking lot," I pointed out). Large numbers of these students were from the northeastern United States and, of these, more than a few had attended prep schools. In many cases, Duke provided their first experience riding a city-type transit bus. Although most of these students were raised well, were objectively intelligent and well-mannered, their interactions with staff members would occasionally betray that privilege. For example, during my tenure we initiated a "Safe Rides" van service to provide door-to-door service from dusk to dawn, primarily to complement the bus service which stopped running at one o'clock in the morning. I was involved with this program and was asked in a meeting with students why we limited the service boundaries. I explained that logistically it was impossible to run timely point-to-point vans if the service area was too broad; students requesting the service would experience lengthy delays for the vans to return to campus which would mitigate the safety factor by exposing students to long waits late at night. One student's immediate and conditioned response was that the staff at Duke just didn't care about the students. I'm fairly certain students were saying the same thing when my brother was a student here. I acknowledge that he may have spoken without thinking, as I have confessed to doing myself, but this response was parroted every time student issues were not delivered 100% to the students' satisfaction. Understand that we had created the concept and sold it to the administration, requested a budget, bought vans, hired staff and operated a service all night because our concern was student safety. Even the boundaries had been carefully crafted to consider the most populated areas of off-campus student housing. "Excuse me," I said, "what did you say you got on your SATs," the inference being that despite any quantitative metric to the contrary, that was a fairly stupid thing to say. I promptly adjourned the meeting. Another time, another clueless student: because this program was part of my portfolio, I found myself driving a van from time to time if we were severely short-handed. One night, after working all day at my regular job, I picked up a student and drove her to her off-campus apartment. It is likely that she had had to wait for me, since, as I mentioned, we were very short-handed, and she spent most of the ride complaining about the lousy service and the University's lack of commitment to student safety. As she prepared to get out of the van, I mentioned that, if she had safety concerns, I could walk her to the door, that I could precede her into her apartment and turn on all her lights and that I could ensure that no one else was in the building. "However," I concluded, "at some point you will have to assume responsibility for your own safety. And," I concluded, "it should probably start with your decision to stay out drinking until three o'clock in the morning before heading home." *In loco parentis,* with the emphasis on loco.

It was considerably different working for the city. About forty per cent of the population in Durham is African-American, and they constitute an overwhelming percentage of the transit riders. Ironically, many of them ride the bus to Duke, where they are employed as housekeepers and cafeteria staff. "Cooking and cleaning" was the refrain, "just like on the plantation" (the institution now known as Duke University was founded in Randolph County, North Carolina, in 1838, as Brown's Schoolhouse. By 1859, it had been renamed Trinity College. Trinity College moved to Durham, North Carolina, in 1892. In 1924, James B. Duke founded Duke University, naming it for his family. The bulk of the endowment money for this enterprise came from the sale of bright-leaf tobacco, a high-quality tobacco grown on the Duke plantation, a tobacco which became extremely popular among the soldiers who stopped in Durham while returning home after the Civil War). In Durham, about eighty percent of the passengers were identified as "transit dependent" which meant that only one person in five riding the bus in Durham could afford a transportation option other than the city bus. In most transit systems, Park and Ride availability (parking a car and then boarding a bus for a trip downtown) and BRT (Bus Rapid Transit- buses riding in dedicated express lanes) may offer attractive commuter options. Not so in Durham. Very few professional people rode the bus, unless they were planning to transfer to a regional bus at the terminal. When I first started working for the city, buses were equipped with a recorded message that played "Thank you for choosing DATA" every time the bus stopped to board or alight passengers. On the basis of the aforementioned statistic, I persuaded the marketing folks to change the message to "Thank you for using DATA," since implying they had a choice seemed unnecessarily cruel.

A NOT SO PC DEBUT

I nitially, I spent a good deal of time in the dispatch office. This was a logical place for me to start for a couple of reasons. In the first place, it was the first place- the location where operators reported to sign in. This gave me the opportunity to meet the 125 drivers face-to-face and begin to recognize them and to learn their names. Once they reported to the dispatch window, I would check them off the daily run-board, indicating that they had reported for duty and that their run would be covered. In the second place, the management staff was in the building and available for assistance in case a situation arose that I was not yet comfortable handling. If a bus or passenger incident developed, for instance, the Operations Manager was in the next office and could initiate the appropriate procedures. In addition to learning who the operators were, I had yet to learn the staff roles as well. It took some time for me to get accustomed to the frenetic pace in that office, and I never felt comfortable sitting in one spot for an entire shift. I managed to adjust, eventually, but being deskbound was every bit as confining and soul-crushing as I had imagined as a young man first seeking employment.

Monday through Friday DATA operated bus service to the Durham Exchange Club Industries (DECI) twice daily for the benefit of disabled employees who worked there. Most of these workers were sight impaired, but fully capable of handling the repetitive tasks involved in assembly-line manufacturing. The bus would pull to the front door of DECI where a manager would greet them in the morning and to which (s)he would escort them at the end of their shift. This dedicated charter was a bid run- operators could choose this as part of their package of work. After returning these passengers to Durham Station in the afternoon, the drivers would begin their scheduled work for the evening shift. One afternoon I screwed up. The operator assigned to the DECI run failed to report, and I overlooked his absence until I received a panicked call from the manager at the Exchange Club inquiring about the missing bus. A quick check of the run-board indicated my error. After apologizing for my oversight, I assured him that I would have a bus there shortly and sent a spare operator to cover the run. It was time to face the music, though, and with great trepidation I went into the adjacent office to report my lapse to the Ops manager. I explained how I had missed the afternoon DECI run, and had not caught my error until they called. "What did you say to them?" he wanted to know. Had I just explained my apology that would have been the end of it, but I was somewhat flustered so the first thing out of my mouth was a badly-timed joke. "They're blind, so I told them the bus was sitting right outside their front door." "NO, you didn't!" he exclaimed in shock. Of course not. It was an honest mistake made manageable by the presence of a spare operator, but I soon found myself spending less time in the office and more time at the downtown bus terminal. Pretty much a win/win for me, as I definitely preferred being outside.

NIGHT-LIFE IN DURHAM

A s an Operations Supervisor at DATA, one performed a variety of roles: Dispatcher, Road Supervisor, Terminal Supervisor. I worked in these various capacities for about eleven months before becoming the full-time New Operator Trainer, which generated its own "Funny but True" episodes, but it was in the role of Terminal Supervisor where most of the action was. I had not been employed for long, perhaps a month or so, when I got my first taste of downtown at night. It was shortly before midnight- the last pullout of the day before the end of service- when a car pulled into the bus area driving the wrong way around the terminal. Buses at the terminal were directed in a clockwise direction; other vehicles were prohibited from any direction, so I ran after the car to turn him around and instruct him to leave when I heard over my two-way radio that there was a man on the platform with a gun. I immediately changed directions and ran for the Terminal building, where the city police were clearing the building and locking it up for the night. (The city paid to have at least two Durham police officers on duty whenever the terminal was open). I heard a shot, not a pistol shot but a shotgun blast, turned around and noticed everyone else rushing for the safety of the building. The shots were a result of a domestic dispute which the police resolved quickly and handled flawlessly, disarming the shooter and making an arrest with no one getting hurt. Two eye-opening observations were made as a result of that evening, however. The first was the low regard that citizens had for their local bus provider. I heard a ceaseless barrage of complaints that night from passengers who blamed the delays on DATA, even though the terminal had become a crime scene and was closed for a criminal investigation. I explained that what had happened was not a service issue but a community problem, and that our employees were no happier than they were about sitting at the terminal surrounded by crime tape, unable to complete their last runs and go home. The other observation was offered by my sister-in-law in Connecticut, who googled "shots fired at Durham Station" and was surprised to get a page-full of hits. "Where does he work?" she asked my wife the next day. "The O.K Corral?"

DURHAM STATION

T he transit department for the city of Durham makes in excess of half a million passenger-trips a year (or, as I fa-
cetiously interpreted the data- it transports the same five hundred
people, one thousand times a year). No question about it, familiar-
ity could breed contempt, since the people who complained about
the bus service (or the bus employees, the vending machines in
the terminal building, the weather or the landscaping) on Monday
were usually the same people who complained every other day of
the week. Conversely, some passengers were always upbeat. I instructed new trainees to picture our passengers as residing along
a bell-shaped curve where there would be outliers who could be
difficult to deal with, but most of the interactions we had on a
daily basis were with that huge population who fell in the broad
middle of the curve. (I avoided a discussion of standard deviations,
and the differences between the mean, the median and the mode).
Friends were made easily- someone approached with a hard-luck
story- "My dog ate my ticket," for example- and you'd give her a
courtesy ride. This was the simplest way to make a friend, but it
could become habit-forming. Take, for example, the relationship
I had forged with a middle-aged, African-American female drug
user who was very friendly, well-spoken and outgoing. She paid
her fare most days, but when she was using stuff, she sometimes
had no money, and I tended to look after her. One week she had
been short for a couple of days in a row and I made sure she
got home on the bus. One of the operators approached me and
pointed out that I had let her ride for free three times that week.

"I'm flattered that you are paying so much attention to my goings-on around here," I told him, "but I'm doing her. Mind your own business." Crude, but effective. He never questioned my authority again.

The terminal was also the locus for newly released criminals; the Sheriff's Department would bring them to the terminal from the jail conveniently located down the street and drop them off. Greyhound and Mega Bus also provided service from Durham Station, but from time to time a newly-released criminal would arrive needing a local bus home. One day, a young man covered in prison tattoos including on his shaved skull asked me to put him on a bus so he could get home. We exchanged brief pleasantries and I mentioned my own tattoo, which I claimed said "I survived Auschwitz and all I got was this lousy tattoo." When he asked me what that meant, I apologized and explained that I misinterpreted his embrace of Aryan symbols for some basic understanding of their significance. "Never mind, it was before your time, of course you wouldn't get it. Let's just get you on the bus." I then asked the bus operator if she would kindly take my son home with a courtesy pass, since he had just been released from jail and had no money. You should have seen the look on her face as she processed my request. She may still allow this young man to ride for free, thinking she is doing me, and my son, a big favor.

After the buses departed Durham Station, there was a lull until the next buses would roll up in a half-hour. I'd try to find an uninhabited bench and sit until they arrived, happy to be off my feet for a bit. One day, a passenger spied me sitting there doing nothing and came up to me. "How do I get a job like that?" he inquired. That's typically intended as an insult, a clue that one resents a city employee sitting down on the job, so I may have been a tad defensive when I responded, "Get fifty years of experience in the transportation industry." "Oh," he responded, momentarily abashed. Then, for emphasis I added, "By the way, it would help if you knew someone."

BEAT IT

His sex life was like a Ferrari. He didn't have one of those, either.

It was still very early in my tenure when I took advantage of a beautiful spring night and went for a stroll around the terminal shortly after the buses had cleared the platform. As I got to the farthest reaches of the city property, I came face-to-face with a guy whose own equipment had cleared its platform, was out and was being driven hard. As the British might say, "he was having a bit of a wank."

"Put it away," I instructed. I doubt it was modesty as he turned his back and walked away from me, without missing a beat.

"Put it away," I repeated. He turned to face me, still stroking away.

"Hey man, (stroke) what are you (stroke) all up in my face for (stroke)?"

"I am not 'up in your face.' I am telling you that what you are doing is against the law. And pretty nasty, by the way."

"You don't (stroke) need to be all up in my face (stroke)."

"I'm trying to cut you a break. If you don't stop, I'm going to get the cops out here."

"Go away and leave me alone (stroke, stroke)."

"Okay," I said. "Have it your way." With that, I keyed the mike and requested the police meet me on the platform. As they approached, my friend turned and walked away, trying to recapture the rapture. The cops, satisfied to have chased this miscreant off the property retreated to the comforts of the terminal building. It would appear that in our community it is only illegal to masturbate on public property; safely off the city grounds any pervert is free to pursue his pleasures without the hassle of law enforcement "getting all up in one's face."

While we're on the subject of gross bodily functions and law enforcement, let me clue you in on a nasty trick that apparently is in favor among a certain (low) class of law-breakers. For the squeamish, you may wish to skip this paragraph. I was working at the Terminal one evening when I received a call from one of the on-duty cops to meet them in the back corner of the property where we parked our company vehicles. I arrived to the sight of a derelict individual and a request to escort this individual to the jail for booking. I immediately denied the request because said derelict individual had completely soiled himself and was stand-ing wearing only his handcuffs and a creamy layer of his own ex-crement. "You have to take us," said the cops, "it's your job." After ascertaining that it actually was the supervisor's job to assist the hired security with escorts to the jail, I insisted that I would need a minute or two to get ready. I went inside the building and located the housekeeping supply closet and helped myself to a liberal number of plastic garbage bags- enough to wallpaper the inside of my company car. I opened all of the windows and got everyone in the car and delivered them down the street to the electric gate of the jailhouse. The two policemen started to get out of the car, before I asked them if maybe they weren't forgetting something. "Oh, yeah, thanks Chris." "Not what I meant, guys, don't forget your garbage bags." You have to draw the line somewhere.

THE TRUANT

One morning the policeman on duty asked me if I would do him a favor and deliver a twelve-year-old truant to school. It seemed pointless, since I recognized him as a fixture at the terminal and could not assure the cop that he would attend class after I dropped him off, but I agreed. While walking over to my car, the truant child asked me why he had to go to school and I explained that it would broaden his horizons. When he asked me what the f---- I was talking about I asked him if it was "broaden" or "horizons" that threw him. Since I always listened to classical music when I drove (try having road rage listening to Mozart, was my argument), the music came on when I started the car and he asked me "What is this shit?" "This, my young friend, is the answer to your last question," I said. "This is classical music, and listening to it will broaden your horizons." "Turn this shit off," was his pithy rejoinder. "You probably aren't aware," I continued, "that Mozart had composed half a dozen symphonies by the time he was your age." Feigning nonchalance at this little tidbit, he replied that he didn't need school because he made more money than I did. I agreed that he made a good argument; that despite his genius and prolific production of timeless music, Mozart had died poor because he didn't sell drugs at the opera house. I also explained that since I worked in public transportation, everyone made more money than I did; hence, I could not be impressed with his earning prowess. I also mentioned that I had a life even when the bus terminal was closed. I pulled up to his Middle School and dropped him off, then left without seeing if he headed indoors because I already knew what his intentions were. Since I was going to stop and get coffee, I expected him to beat me back downtown.

THE VIETNAM VETERAN

O ne of the first lessons learned as a transit employee was how many people paid my salary. A daily refrain I heard was "You have to (supply the operative verb) because I pay your salary." In most cases this was amusing, because, if you bothered to explain the whole taxes thing to them, they would see that they had it backwards. So much of this 80% transit-dependent bus-riding population received some form of government assistance that those of us who were employed and paid taxes were actually subsidizing them, essentially paying *their* salaries, but this was an argument better left unarticulated. The other thing one learned was the sense of entitlement that a number of these same individuals felt, possibly as a result of walking into a government office and receiving this largesse. I did try to explain, from time to time, that we, as a contract service provider, could only provide as much service as the budget controlled by the city allowed. "Why don't you have more buses on the road?" for example. Or, "why is that spare bus sitting over there, with no driver in it?" Thank you all for illustrating my point. "Our annual budget allows us to employ x number of drivers, and to operate y amount of buses, and because you are paying my salary instead of paying your taxes you are not contributing to these operating costs, consequently, we are limited in what we can do." The truth is, public transportation in every district operates at a deficit. The unit cost of moving a passenger in Durham is, let's say, ten dollars. The fare in Durham for an all-day pass, good for any bus, on any route, is two dollars. The fare has not increased in Durham for fifteen years (like the cost of a hot dog and a drink at Costco) but every cost associated with providing that service has increased. Students in Durham ride free to the age of eighteen, seniors sixty-five and older ride free, and Medicare/Medicaid recipients are eligible for reduced (half-price) bus tickets. (This is a popular scam. Any number of people could be found at the terminal with walkers, wheelchairs or electric scooters until the day they boarded the bus without their mobility device. When asked what happened, they would typically respond, "I don't need it anymore!" Miracle cure at Lourdes? Of course not. "I qualified!" (for benefits) they would proudly proclaim, to any of the saps within hearing distance who still had to pay full fare).

Another scam was the fraudulent practice of pass-backs. People would board the bus and swipe an all-day pass, then turn around and hand that pass to a friend who would use it on a different bus. Operators were instructed not to challenge this practice because it was counterproductive to involve our drivers with this type of fare hassle, since disputes like these slowed the boarding process and often escalated. Escalation would then require intervention by a supervisor, and sometimes the involvement of police to remove recalcitrant passengers, which resulted in a busload of angry and late passengers. When the object is to maintain a schedule and keep the passengers happy, this is not a sustainable business model; better to eat the loss and keep the system functioning. Without our own influx of government assistance, we would have to park the buses. All of this, incidentally, is prelude to an introduction to some of my most intransigent passengers.

Service complaints arose daily. These situations required patience and skill which I possessed in abundance, but disbursed modestly. Remember, my personal curriculum vitae included a long history of real-life experience sitting in traffic, driving in bad weather, detouring around accidents and through construction, suffering flat tires and mechanical failures, so if anyone understood the vagaries of the transportation industry it was I. Try explaining that to a group of frustrated ticket-holders standing in bad weather with a reasonable expectation of having their bus show up on time. The shoe was on the other foot now. Two things were capable of evaporating my patience, however, personal/profane attacks, and even worse, a remorseless lack of logic.

DATA had what is called hub-and-spoke service, with the hub being the downtown terminal, or Durham Station. All service emanated from this hub and served the spokes, which were the routes that went out to end-points before turning around and returning downtown. For the sake of convenience, let's assume every roundtrip was one hour, with one-half hour outbound to the end of the line and one-half hour back to downtown. Since buses departed every half-hour during the daytime, we needed to deploy multiple buses on each route. Late buses were a critical operational flaw, then, since many passengers had to ride two or more buses to get to their destination, (those Duke employees, for example, might need a bus downtown before boarding the bus for Duke) and late buses meant missed connections. A bus that was only a few minutes late could mean an extra half-hour wait for the next one. So, yes, frustration came with the territory; I understood this and I tried to deal with it sympathetically. The biggest problems existed at rush hour. Big systems deploy more vehicles during peak hours, but we did not have that luxury. When asked why the five o'clock bus was late, for instance, I could only answer that it was rush hour, and when it was pointed out that this same bus was late every day, I could only state the obvious- "rush hour always happens at this time of day." I wished I had a better answer, or more buses, and more drivers.

One afternoon, hot and humid and miserable, there were about fifteen people waiting for the bus, which, of course, was stuck in traffic. Everyone was complaining loudly, and I asked them to please speak one at a time and I would try to address each of their concerns. One gentleman spoke over everyone, and would not let anyone else get a word in. He was a Vietnam veteran, and kept insisting that, as such, he shouldn't have to put up with this. I tried my best, honestly. I told him that we appreciated his military service and suggested that it was likely that he got treated poorly when he returned home. I turned my attention to someone else but the vet wouldn't let up. "I don't have to put up with this!" he shouted again. I told him that, unfortunately, until his bus arrived, or, unless he chose to walk to his destination, he had no choice but to put up with it, like everyone else. On and on he went, with the same argument. I felt myself starting to lose it. "Sir, I understand your argument if you're making it at the Veterans' Hospital, for example, or perhaps at Social Services, where your service really might define your benefit, but can you explain to me how your military service overseas fifty years ago has any bearing whatsoever on how buses operate in Durham today?" If I thought I could woo him with logic, I was mistaken, he was too worked up. Again, the same argument about the entitlement he felt that he deserved- he had served his country in Vietnam, so dammit, where was his bus? I tried one more time before giving up, he was too angry and beyond reason. As I turned to walk away, I left him with this thought- "Maybe you should have gone to Canada, sir, instead of Vietnam. My understanding is that the buses are always on time there."

The only conclusion that I could draw from these interactions was that some people are bereft of the logic gene. Like my soldier friend, a similar set of circumstances betrayed a different passenger's absence of this gene. On Sundays, the bus schedule is abbreviated, with hourly service only, and the first departure from Durham Station at seven o'clock in the morning. Shortly after seven, a passenger approached me and complained that his driver was not in the bus. I explained that the terminal building is locked until seven, and it was likely that the operator had run inside to use the rest room. He exclaimed that it was poor customer service and why would we even hire individuals who could not adhere to the bus schedules. I explained with a straight face that our hiring process was designed to screen out drivers who have bodily functions, but some slip through the cracks. There is almost no chance of a late bus on Sundays, since there is very little traffic and few stops need to be made because of the scarcity of passengers until much later in the day. "I don't have to put up with this!" he shouted, echoing the bizarre and completely absurd complaint of the Vietnam vet. Why, yes, I always wanted to say, of course you have to put up with this, sir or ma'am, those of us with a clue call it reality. "This is ridiculous," he shouted again. And he really was shouting, although it was just the two of us in the stillness of a quiet, and heretofore peaceful, early Sunday morning. When he closed his mouth you could hear birds. "Okay," I offered, knowing that I would regret asking the question. "Why don't you have to put up with this?" "My brother," he explained, giving me his best, completely logical answer why he didn't have to put up with this, "is a big shot at ABC and makes a quarter of a million dollars a year!" Dangerously climbing out on a very tenuous limb, I suggested that maybe, if that was the case, mightn't it be more likely that his brother was the one who wouldn't have to put up with it, since, in all likelihood, he could probably afford a car? "In the absence of your well-paid brother buying you a car of your own, I'm afraid you are going to have to put up with this, and wait until my operator finishes his business in the bathroom." Missing operator accounted for, late departure explained, argument over, complaint resolved. Next case.

THE REMORSEFUL SMOKER

T he city of Durham has an ordinance prohibiting smoking on any of its properties. The staff was generally inclined to look the other way, but I tried to enforce it by directing smokers to an area provided for them on the corner of the property. This led to a panoply of responses, the most benign a simple thank you, (Them- "Thank you. I didn't know that." And me, thinking, right. It's the third time I've told this guy this week.) There were "No Smoking" signs posted at every gate, so sometimes I would ask them simply to stand a little closer to the sign while they finished their cigarette. "Why?" they wondered. "Just humor me, okay? It makes a great tableau." Mostly, I could anticipate one of two responses- either the, "Sure, no problem," or "What kind of asshole are you?" categories (with the occasional "What's a tab-blow?" thrown in). I always hoped for the latter because I had a ready response. I would look at them and say, "You really want to know what kind of ass- hole am I? I'm the kind of asshole who determines if you ride the bus or if you walk home. So, what's it going to be?" But one rainy morning I got quite a different response. This from a man carrying an umbrella and with a small child in tow. Sticking the point of his umbrella within inches of my nose, he threatened to put the cigarette out in my face. Without flinching, and with the umbrella still in my face I said, "If you're trying to impress your child, do whatever you need to do, but I assure you that if you manage to pull that off, we're talking jail time." By now, a policeman, alerted by radio from one of the buses, had sauntered over and asked me what was going on. I explained the situation and when asked how I would like him to handle it, I suggested that he could escort the gentleman off the property. "I don't believe he should be riding the bus with that attitude." And that was that, so I thought.

As it happened, and unbeknownst to me, the police had then trespassed him from the property and given him a thirty-day exclusion from the system, for communicating a threat. I would have been okay with a one-day ban, since I understood that people have bad days, and with the population of passengers we served, so many of them chronically broke, self-medicated and miserable, I was not surprised to encounter them on a regular basis. I was taken aback then, a couple of days later, when the Risk Manager at work called me into his office to let me know that this same gentleman had called seeking redress. His plaint, it seems, was that he needed the bus because he currently had no other means of transportation. As the Risk Manager was taking his information and jotting down some notes for his incident report, he asked for the speaker's name. "John," he answered. "Last name?" "Smith." (Not this guy's real name). "Well, Mr. Smith," intoned the Risk Manager, "unfortunately the man you threatened would have been your trainer in the next new-operator class." "Would have been?" he asked. Believe it or not, this guy with the kid and the umbrella and the cigarette and the miserable attitude had been recently interviewed by the Risk Manager and conditionally hired to start training as a bus operator in the next class. It was his misfortune that one of the conditions of employment was not to extinguish cigarettes in the faces of future co-workers. I gave this man all the credit in the world, though, for his behavior after the fact. He recognized me at a bus stop a couple of months later, approached me and said he needed to apologize. "What for?" I asked, because I did not remember him. "I threatened to put a cigarette out in your face," he confessed, "and I was wrong." I told him that it took a big man to accept the fact that extinguishing burning cigarettes on human flesh was wrong, and that I appreciated his apology. I did wonder if he thought it was wrong because people are not supposed to be that crazy aggressive or because it had cost him a potential job. In either case, I did not feel compelled to inform him that we would not be reevaluating his application.

MY COUNTRY, TSK, TSK ON THEE"

O ne of our regular passengers was a recovering heroin addict who was known to me only by his nickname, "Country." Country was an anomaly, a rare but ubiquitous Caucasian presence at the bus terminal, always in his wheelchair, bumming cigarettes while waiting to get to the methadone clinic or the Social Services office. As ornery as he could get, I cut him a lot of slack because, why else, he was a recovering heroin addict in a wheelchair. I'm not the easiest person to be around and I'm blessed with good health, was never addicted to heroin and I own a car. I certainly would have had an attitude if I had been in his shoes. But that, you see, was the problem and the source of the friction between us; Country didn't always wear shoes, or a shirt for that matter, and he wore the skimpiest cut-off jeans that left a lot of exposed skin. This was problematic because his skin was covered with ulcerating sores. Operators did not want to board him, because the requirement to strap down his wheelchair put them into direct contact with his exposed skin, so I often got called to mediate. I would have to explain that he couldn't get on the bus without shoes or a shirt. He would argue for a while and finally admit that he had a shirt in a wicker basket attached to the back of his wheelchair. "Just hand it to me, and I'll put it on" he'd say. "No way am I sticking my hand in that basket," I'd aver. "I don't know what's in there and, even if I did, I wouldn't put my hand in it. If something went missing, you'd blame me." This annoyed him to the point where he refused to cooperate any further. "Fine, no shirt, no service for you today." He became bellicose the first time he heard this, commencing with a stream of profanity that rivaled the best I had heard from truckers and longshoremen. I told him he could holler all he wanted, but I was not going to tolerate his obscenities and walked away. He followed immediately behind me in his motorized wheelchair, still screaming names at me. "You know what you are?" he bellowed. "You're a (insert the "N" word here). I stopped and turned around. "Really? That's the best you can do? You should be ashamed of yourself." With that I set off at a fairly rapid pace with hm in pursuit. Looking over my shoulder and seeing him maintaining his distance behind me I cut between some shrubs; he plowed right over them. Stopping once more, I turned to him and told him that I was going into the terminal building and that I was going to climb the stairs halfway up to the second floor. If he wanted to scream at me, he could take the elevator upstairs, but by the time he got there I would be gone. He finally submitted, but did not ride the bus that day. We actually suspended his privileges for thirty days, but he was back the next morning thanks to the intervention of his case worker at Social Services.

SWEET LAND OF INEQUITY

In Durham, one thing that is as common at intersections as a stop signal is a person with a sign pleading for monetary assistance. ("Beggar" sounds so louche). Country was one of these people and he had staked out a good spot near a very busy intersection. There was a narrow, raised traffic island separating east and west lanes, and he would sit with his sign on this concrete island and solicit. One day I had a busload of trainees and we stopped at the light right next to the island. I watched as Country maneuvered his wheelchair too close to the edge and tipped over, as if in slow motion, spilling into the street. I yelled at the trainee driving the bus to pull the emergency brake, put on the hazard lights and open the door. I jumped out, ran around the bus and lifted Country out of the street and onto the island and stopped the incoming traffic to rescue his wheelchair. Meanwhile, a good Samaritan driving towards us stopped and got out of her car. "Is he all right?" she wanted to know. My adrenalin-fueled response? "He's fine. He performs this routine all day long because he thinks it evokes sympathy and increases the likelihood that people will stop and give him money." "Really?" the Samaritan wanted to know. "No, not really," I said. "He just got too close to the edge and fell over. Thank you for stopping." I got back in the bus and we left when the light changed.

BUSMAN'S HOLIDAY

M y wife and I traveled to California for the wedding of our nephew in the Bay area and decided to stay and do the tourist thing. Given my occupation, we decided to park our rental car and buy weekly bus passes. It could not have been more convenient as we were in a downtown hotel with a bus stop mere steps from the front door. With the exception of a day spent on the Monterey peninsula, we traveled almost exclusively on the city bus and, other than one hellish trip, the bus experience was completely stress-free. The problem, as I might have anticipated, is that, even in San Francisco, a little rain could fall. In this set of circumstances, it was more like a reign of terror perpetrated by one very miserable individual.

Aboard the bus was a class of young and incredibly adorable students who were clearly on an outing of some kind. They were mostly Asian-Americans, smartly dressed in school uniforms, and quite excited about their field trip. I think most of the passengers enjoyed having these children on the bus and were sharing in their enthusiasm. There is one in every group, however... One individual who was not sharing their joy about being on the bus instead of in the classroom was an angry young man sitting in the back, who began shouting at the kids, hurling numerous profanities at them. "SHUT THE F____ UP!!" he repeated, over and over. I kept waiting for the operator to say something. In our system, profanity would get you thrown off the bus, but the driver said nothing, obviously hoping the individual was nearing his destination and would get off. I, on the other hand, was not so patient.

Because I had taken a three-day seminar on managing anger and learning de-escalation skills, and because I had so much practice putting what I had learned to use, and because I can be an impulsive idiot and act without thinking, I stood up and confronted the young man. "Hey, man, chill. They're just little kids, how about giving them a break." (That went well, I thought). "DO YOU WANT TO DIE?" he screamed. My wife started whispering for me to sit down. "No, I don't, but can't you consider the other passengers on the bus? The situation is a little uncomfortable." "HAVE YOU EVER SEEN DEAD PEOPLE?" he shouted. My wife was now yanking on my arm and beseeching me to sit down. We went back and forth like this for a bit, with every threat and consequent rejoinder getting us nearer to the denouement, which could not come soon enough. Part of his situation, it arose, was that it was his birthday (which I assumed he had begun celebrating early, perhaps early the night before) and he didn't feel he should have to "...put up with all this shit because it was giving him a headache." Hmm, where had I heard that before? I kept him busy threatening me instead of the schoolkids until they got off, at which point I turned around and sat down. He continued his threatening harangue behind my back until he, too, got off the bus, at which time a number of the passengers approached me to thank me for my intervention. My wife remarked what a nice gesture that was, but I wondered where they had all been when I needed them.

ACCIDENTS DO HAPPEN

W hen we did not have a training class in session, it was customary for me to be deployed around our service area as a trouble-shooter. This might have been to mediate disputes, to help direct or control traffic or to conduct accident investigations, of which I had a fair bit of experience. In the 1990s I spent three different weeks at the Transportation Safety Institute in Oklahoma City, taking courses in Accident Investigation, and much of my time at Duke was spent working with the Risk Management group. The difference between Duke and the city transit systems could not have been more pronounced when it came to passengers' attitudes about accidents. Duke students, for the most part, could not be bothered- they had classes to get to, so they would leave the scene and hustle off. Or, realizing that they might be called to testify at a future trial if they claimed an injury or made a statement, they typically swore off medical assistance and remained mute witnesses. Passengers on city transit buses, on the other hand, lived for the opportunity to score big in a settlement with the city. When I first went to work for the city, their insurance carrier had the philosophy that it was cheaper to pay a claim than to go to court, particularly since the juries of their peers often seemed sympathetic to passengers. This may have been a sound strategy initially, but over the years a mindset developed that the city was vulnerable and citizens came to understand that any reasonable claim could produce a settlement check. During late autumn of my first year, I noticed a sizeable increase in the number of claims. When I pointed this out to the Risk Manager, he simply pointed out to me that "Christmas is coming, and people need their checks. It happens every year." This practice led to some creatively fraudulent claims, some of the funnier but true ones I have detailed below.

TWO NECK INJURIES

One time a young pregnant woman reported to me that she had slammed into the back of the seat in front of her when the bus was hit by another vehicle, and she insisted on taking an ambulance to the Emergency Department to check the status of her unborn child. Her warning to me was something to the effect that she would own the bus company if anything was wrong with her child. I did not begrudge her a status check, since I doubted that she made routine maternity visits and, at the very least, a doctor might counsel her about her unhealthy daily habits. What a number of these passengers failed to realize was that on-board cameras, strategically placed, recorded everything that happened (or didn't happen) on the bus. One thing that clearly did not happen to this young lady was any harm to her unborn child. You see, she was sitting in one of the perimeter seats (seats that face the aisle, not the front of the bus) so there was no seat in front of her to cause her any harm. Many claims were resolved simply by inviting the plaintiffs' lawyers to our offices to review the taped recordings of their clients claimed injuries, with many of these lawyers thanking us for sparing them the expense and humiliation of a trial. In this particular case, the city was spared the ignominy of transferring ownership of the bus company to the aggrieved young lady and her progeny for her pain and suffering.

One morning a young man approached me at the terminal and explained that he had been riding on the bus whose front tire had blown out, and he needed to report an injury to his neck sustained as a result of this blowout. This was fairly routine- a minor accident, an injury claim and hopefully some form of compensation. I replied that the tire incident had not yet been reported to me, but I gave him a form to fill out. After he went inside to complete his report, I called the dispatcher about the blow out, and learned that it had been a front airbag that had blown, not a tire. Buses with air-ride suspensions ride on bags or bellows full of air instead of shock absorbers or springs, and from time to time these bags wear out and pop like a balloon from their internal pressure. This is what had happened in my victim's case- a loud bang, perhaps, but unlikely to cause any injury, particularly a front airbag blowout causing injury to a passenger sitting in the rear of the bus. A loud noise, indeed, but we're talking about a drop of a few inches forty-five feet away from our victim, difficult, really, to distinguish from hitting a pothole. When he returned with his paperwork, a fellow compensation-seeker was in tow claiming the same injury from the same blowout. I gave this second young man a form, repeated the instructions and sent them both back inside. When they returned, I took both copies and read them over. "Your statements similarly claim that while you were riding along you heard a loud bang, there was 'a big jerk' in the back of the bus and then your necks immediately started to hurt. Do I have that right?" "Yes," they agreed, "that's exactly what happened." "So" I probed, "would it be fair to say that since you both sustained injuries when the tire went flat there were actually two big jerks in the back of the bus" They looked at me quizzically, then at each other and then back at me. "Yes, that's right. That's what happened." Me- "Thanks, guys. That's all I need. I'll go ahead and file this paperwork."

New transit management brought with it a change in insurers and a dramatic change in philosophy. The new strategy (and one most of us with health insurance will recognize) was to deny every claim and let the injured party attempt to prove damages. This did not stop the flow of passengers requesting medical attention or unnecessary hospital visits to bolster a claim, but, adding insult to phantom injury, a litigant losing their case would henceforth be banned from the system for attempting to commit fraud against the city. Of course, these changes took some time to enter into public consciousness, so we still had to deal with characters like the two big jerks above, and the poor fellow I describe next.

CASE CLOSED

One scenario that occurred with disturbing frequency were buses that got struck from behind while making a service stop. I was never surprised because experience had taught me that people do not really drive when they operate their cars- by that I mean they do not focus on the task of driving; driving well takes concentration, effort and skill. I'm comfortable saying most people think that they can multitask while operating a three-thousand-pound vehicle at any speed. A landmark study from the early 2000's has been reexamined frequently in the intervening years and still holds up. Briefly, this study showed that drivers on phones (either hand-held or hands-free) took more time and traveled greater distances before stopping than a control group, or even by subjects who were legally impaired. The term of choice is "distraction blindness" which describes one's inability to fully concentrate on two activities at one time. Studies also confirm the risk of not paying attention: driving while distracted increases your "risk-opportunity" (the odds of *committing an unsafe maneuver* like an unintended lane deviation) by a factor of six, and increases your odds of *actually having an accident* by a factor of four). To put it more succinctly, distracted drivers have the exact same increased risk of having an accident as an impaired driver, and, raise your hand if you believe that more drunk drivers on the road would improve highway safety. Anecdotal studies put the number of operators using cell-phones while driving close to 50%. If these studies are anywhere near accurate, this means that almost half of the drivers on the road at any one time drive with the same risk to you as drunk drivers. Sobering thought.

Since I am a community-minded citizen, I did not object when my services were volunteered by an acquaintance to get drunk for the Sherriff's Department. Allow me to amplify. The department was training a new class of deputies and the determination had been made to illustrate the "Standardized Field Sobriety Test" with actual drunk people. I had some friends in the Police Department who asked if I would mind getting drunk, and undergo the testing that police conduct if they suspect an operator of impairment. Because there were rarely times when I minded getting drunk, I showed up at the community college where the training was to take place at the appointed hour, was offered my drink of choice (George Dickel Tennessee whiskey) and began to drink to inebriation. We submitted to periodic breathalyzer tests to ensure that we were over the legal limit and, when we hit the magic number (0.08 Blood Alcohol Content (BAC)), we underwent the testing. For the uninitiated, roadside sobriety testing consists of three facets- horizontal gaze nystagmus (HGN), which involves following an object (like a pen) with your eyes from side to side while keeping your head straight; the walk and turn, where the subject is directed to take nine steps, touching heel-to-toe, along a straight line, turning on one foot and returning in the same manner; and the one leg stand which involves standing on one leg for thirty seconds with the other leg raised six inches off the ground. (Disclosure: I can no longer perform this last exercise even while sober due to balance issues associated with a condition my doctors describe as vestibular neuritis, but which I refer to by its generic name- getting old). Of course, newly minted officers are also trained to observe obvious physical signs such as posture and speech. It was a remarkable evening spent drinking with friends under very strange circumstances, concluding with an escort home, with my son announcing my arrival with "Mom! Dad's getting out of a police car."

Because the buses were city property, policy dictated that

any and all accidents had to be reported. So, when a woman pulled out to pass a stopped bus and broke her passenger-side mirror on the back corner of the bus, the operator properly called it in. The woman drove away from the scene leaving behind her broken mirror but there was no damage to the bus; contact, however brief and inconsequential, had been made. When I arrived at the scene most of the passengers were unaware that the bus had been struck, until I explained that I was there to file an accident report. Of course, making that announcement caused injury complaints to cascade, including a few requests for EMS technicians and, in one case, a trip to the hospital. I chatted briefly with a number of passengers as I took their contact information (you may or may not be surprised how many people call after the fact to try to get their name on the passenger/injury list) including a young man who had been unaware that a car had even made contact with the bus, but wanted to make sure that I included his name, address and phone number on my report. A month or so later, this young man approached me at the terminal and asked if I remembered him.

"Sure", I said, "we spoke briefly after that accident."

"Yes, I haven't got my check yet."

"Well, these things take time. Be patient, it's only been a couple of weeks."

Another month passed and he sought me out a second time. "You know, I'm still waiting for my check."

I told him that it was out of our hands at that point, that it had been turned over to the insurance company and they would be handling all of the claims. "Your best bet is to have your lawyer call them directly and ask about the status of the claim."

"My lawyer?" he asked.

"Yes, didn't you contact a lawyer to begin a claim against the city to recover damages suffered in the accident?

"No," he responded, "I don't have a lawyer."

"Do you still have your documentation from the hospital," I wanted to know. "Or from any doctor visits you made as a result of the accident?"

"I didn't go to the hospital."

Me- "Did you suffer any injuries that required a doctor's attention?"

Him- "No."

"So, you thought that the city was just going to mail you a check because you were on the bus?"

"Well, yes, isn't that what happens?" I had to explain that the checks were sent to settle claims. Oftentimes, any payments made were simply to cover doctor bills. No claim, no check. Maybe next time," I said sympathetically. The good news for him is that he was not banned from the bus for attempting to commit fraud against the city.

THE AMBASSADOR

It was the Terminal Supervisor's responsibility to ensure that all buses left on time, and, it was likewise their duty to deal with the consequences when this did not happen. Periodically, though, they were thrust into emergency duty as a bus driver if the assigned operator failed to show up. My debut in this capacity was not terribly auspicious. Although I had to learn all of the routes when I started training new operators, I did not know them by heart initially because I had not gone through the operator training program. The philosophy of putting bus routes together fell to the city Transportation Department, and it was fairly well thought out. The buses were made available to those people (primarily those four out of five transit-dependent people) who were most likely to need the bus. It probably goes without saying then, that I was often driving through some fairly depressed (and depressing) parts of town. When I described these neighborhoods to my friends, they questioned my safety but I tended to blow off their concerns. "Before I got this job," I'd assure them, "the only time I went into those areas was to buy crack."

As a former LVO (long vehicle operator), I could handle the bus well enough but I wasn't properly equipped for dealing with passengers or making service stops. Consequently, as I departed the terminal on my maiden voyage with a bus full of people, I drove right past the first couple of stops. A chorus of angry voices from behind me questioned my intelligence, my hearing and my heritage as I had ignored the "Stop Requested" bell. "Sorry," I yelled over my shoulder, "I was only trained how to drive the bus, we never really worked on stopping." My confession threw them a bit but seemed to calm them down, and I began to listen carefully for the bell. The problem, as I confessed, was that I did not really know where all the turns were. At one point, I put on my left turn signal and moved into the left lane when a voice from the back called out, informing me that the next turn was actually a right, not a left. "Really?" I yelled out. "Yes, really," the voice answered. I decided to trust the voice, because these were not mischievous school kids, but mostly adult passengers who were always in too much of a hurry to lead me astray. I managed from there and arrived at the end of the line, where the owner of the voice came up and asked me if I could find my way back to Durham Station. "Yes, thanks, I've got it," I told him, but after observing my performance he suggested that perhaps he would ride back downtown with me, just to make sure.

It turns out that this person was a former bus operator with a somewhat sketchy employment history, who now spent his days as an unpaid "ambassador" for the city assisting with informational requests at Durham Station. He had worked at one time for DATA, as well as other local transit properties, but he seemed to stay in trouble with management. The last straw was when his part-time hustle was exposed. He advertised his services as a charter operator, and would schedule charters for church or family outings on weekends, when the business offices were closed. Then he would "borrow" an idle city transit bus to operate his charter. The city frowned on this unauthorized use of their property and terminated him. The story around more senior drivers who had worked with him was that he would request excessive amounts of bereavement leave, frequently invoking his mother as the deceased. Cognizant of this history, I was skeptical when he told me one day that his mother had passed away, and he was collecting money for her funeral. It sounded like a scam. "Again?" I wanted to ask. But no, I took the high road and offered my condolences for his loss. Then, because I couldn't help it, I asked him if he was planning to "borrow" a hearse.

CODA

As it happens, my desire to "give back to my community" was not simply an obsequious expression of purpose in a job interview, but one of the most enlightening and fulfilling endeavors I had ever pursued. My original plan had been to work for the city for a couple of years, earn a small pension and retire, but I so enjoyed the work that I lingered. There was much to like. As a staunch union guy, I loved the fact that the workers were protected by the Amalgamated Transit Union; collective bargaining with the ATU (in North Carolina, of all places) provided excellent pay and benefits to a group that had historically found the path to the middle class convoluted and confounding. Since North Carolina was an open shop state (employees were protected by the union but were not obligated to join), I invited the union officers into my training classes to educate new drivers about the benefits of membership and made them aware of my own history as a lifelong Teamster. Mostly though, I delighted in the small, funny but true things that happened so routinely from the almost "sitcom-like" contradictions of an old northern white dude working in an environment of mostly young, southern African-Americans. I was constantly learning. One day, while outdoors instructing a class on the proper way to perform a pre-trip inspection, one of my young students pointed to the massive bus tires and said "check out the dubs!" Everyone laughed except me, because I was clueless, and the reference to the oversize tires and rims that were so fashionable with younger drivers had gone right over my head.

The roster of bus operators, characters all, kept me constantly entertained, and taught me much about myself. Right off the bat one of the operators told me that I looked like the actor Harrison Ford. My instantaneous reply: "I get it. We all look alike to you." Was he offended by my reversal of an old white trope? No, in fact he laughed and "Harrison Ford" became my moniker for the remainder of my tenure. One day he yelled out this nickname across the terminal platform to get my attention and I approached him, this hugely muscled weight-lifting gym rat half my age with biceps bigger around than my thighs, and told him if he ever called me that in front of passengers again, I was going to kick his ass. The damage had been inflicted, however, as he had been overheard and passengers began to call me that as well; one hummed the theme song from "Indiana Jones" whenever he saw me.

One of the more charismatic operators that I had the pleasure to work with also referred to me as Harrison, and I called him Darryl, because he bore such a strong resemblance to Darryl Strawberry, the former New York Mets and the Yankees center-fielder. "Darryl," as I'll refer to him, was a New Yorker himself, from Bedford-Stuyvesant, the projects in Brooklyn, where he, like many of his contemporaries, had had some minor issues with the law as a teenager. Darryl was bright enough to understand his limited options if he remained in New York, so he gathered his family and moved south. Over the years he brought his nieces and nephews down to live with him, assembling, at last count, about two dozen relatives under his protective wings. I was unaware of this family dynamic until his funeral when the extended family entered the church and sat, en masse, in the front rows, and someone explained their presence to me. Did I mention his charisma? Darryl continued to work as he battled cancer, working through the debilitating effects of radiation and chemotherapy treatments when he had the strength. I asked him about this commitment to work and he claimed that it was what was keeping him alive; staying home was not an option. He was so inspirational there would have been no excuse for me to miss his funeral. The funeral was well-attended and the church was packed; his family, as I mentioned, occupied most of the first two rows. I learned certain details about Darryl from the guests who came forward to eulogize him, including one of his ex-wives who amused the assembled guests when she introduced herself as "wife #3, from New York." "How many other ex-wives are here?" she wondered. We chuckled when a couple of hands went up. I noticed his girlfriend, another bus driver standing in the back of the church, and wondered how many hands would have gone up if wife #3 had asked, instead, for a show of hands from ex-girlfriends in attendance. Darryl had been busy- all of this love he had managed to share in his brief forty-seven years was being returned by those he had touched and had come to say goodbye.

When the funeral concluded and the recessional began, an older black female approached me and said, "You're Chris, right?" "Yes", I replied. "How did you know my name?"
"From the terminal" she answered.
"Okay, but I'm sorry. I don't remember you from the terminal. What were the circumstances of our meeting?"
"Oh," she replied, unabashed. "We never met."
My curiosity was piqued. "I give up. How do you know me from the terminal, then?"
"Easy," she said, confirming what I had long suspected, "You're the white guy." I was not merely Chris, some random white guy who worked for DATA, but Chris, THE white guy at the bus terminal. However benign I attempted to make my presence felt, I had long understood that I was constantly under the microscope. No matter how many years I was employed at Duke, I could never have achieved status as "the white guy", drowned, as I was, in a sea of similar faces. Perhaps my parochial school education had sunk in after all, as the "do unto others" credo had become part of my internal operating system, and the way I tried to comport myself in public. One day I was engaged in an argument at the terminal that was escalating and becoming quite heated. The aggrieved was becoming very aggressive and I noticed a crowd of young African-American males closing in around us. I managed, finally, to defuse his anger and, as he walked away, the group behind me said, "Don't

worry, Chris, we have your back." It was, quite honestly, one of the most edifying days of my tenure. This exalted yet completely un-earned status was constantly reinforced as passengers would in-variably walk up to me and address their questions and concerns no matter who stood beside me. Most appeared taken aback when I would defer to a colleague and advise them to "ask her, she's in charge." It had taken a very long time for this power of privilege to dawn on me, but this daily experience became an important and unambiguous element in my coming to terms with the advan-tages I enjoyed simply by being both white and male at Durham Station.

The truth is, this could never have been part of my con-sciousness while working at Duke. Working there, my perception of privilege was skewed by the environment around me. I per-ceived as privilege the affordability of $50,000 annual tuitions at a well-respected university, the privilege of expensive cars given as high school graduation gifts, of European ski trips during Spring break and the legacies of generational wealth. Working in downtown Durham forced me to recognize the relativity of this privilege thing. Yes, my car was old, but it ran and it was paid for, plus I could afford the ancillary costs of owning it- registration, insurance and maintenance. Compare that to the reality of people who had difficulty making bus fare every day; folks who would draw out a pocketful of change and ask if I could make up the difference so they could afford to ride, or plead with me to let them take the bus to work so they could pick up their paycheck and pay me back later. It should not have taken me most of a fairly long life and then a few brief years working with these transit-dependent individuals to change my perspective and intuit all the privileges that had been conferred upon me at birth. All of the above funny but true episodes that I have recorded here- the music lessons and ski club trips, concerts, cars, connections and college- had mostly been taken for granted, as my due for having had the good fortune to be born into the middle class. Working in this environment made me acknowledge that these opportunities had accrued to me more as a mere accident of birth, in the DNA I inherited, than to the degree of hard work I had performed thinking that I was earning them. Our employees who drove the buses and the folks who rode them to low-wage jobs worked extremely long hours also but did not enjoy the same benefits of middle-class. The difference between us was primarily my good fortune to have been born holding the cosmic raffle ticket for the Cadillac of genome awards.

AN IRRELEVANT ENDNOTE

A few pages back I referred to the "… 'sitcom-like' contradictions of an old northern white dude working in an environment of mostly young, southern African-Americans" and it got me to thinking. The asymmetry of cultures is a popular device in sitcoms, because the culture-clash formula writes its own jokes. The jokes for the most part seem forced and predictable, based as they are on stereotypes, and are rarely funny, yet they persist. Baby Boomers may remember such a culture-clash in a television series broadcast during the "Golden Age of sitcoms" (I'm kidding, of course- there was never such a thing) on CBS from 1962 to 1971 called "The Beverly Hillbillies". The show featured the Clampetts, a poor backwoods family from the Ozarks who move to Beverly Hills after striking oil on their land. The set-up, you see, put a family of ignorant, cartoonish dolts in the middle of a wealthy, urbane community and watched as highjinks ensued. Does this remind you of anyone or am I the only one who recalls this show and cannot unsee the Trump family? Despite your politics, stay with me for a minute while I explain- you've got this nitwit rube from the sticks (Queens, NY) who lucks into a large sum of money and moves to the big city, where he is clearly out of his element. Our protagonist is a dunce, whose native (lack of) skills do not translate into his new milieu, but he is far too ignorant to understand the embarrassing inappropriateness of his behavior. In the sixties, script writers created an ensemble of like-minded yokels to surround this moron and to provide some laugh-track hilarity, thereby giving us a supporting cast foreshadowing the future First Family, consisting of the mother, a hot-looking eye-candy daughter, and an imbecile son who is rarely separated from his rifle. The supporting cast offers up a weasel-like schemer, a banker, no less, and his secretary (press secretary)? If you're reluctant to buy into my premise, read these actual reviews of the show when it premiered and compare:

- *The New York Times* called the show "**Strained and Unfunny**."
- *Variety* foresaw the future when they wrote, "**Painful to sit through**."
- And the venerable *TV Guide* wrote, in a December 15, 1962 article, "**The whole notion on which "The Beverly Hillbillies is founded is an encouragement to ignorance**."

With that, ladies and gentlemen, I rest my case, and end my book.

PRAISE AND COMMENTS FOR "A TALL TAILOR, TOO" AND ITS AUTHOR

"Dad wrote a book?"   Travis Wardell, son

"Can you believe it?"   Perrie Wardell, son

"It's a cwassic."   Fred Wardell, grandson

"It has chapters and page
  numbers so, maybe it's a book"   Times Book Review

  Nope, never heard of this guy."   Kirkus Review

"Nasty. Total disaster. He's a loser."   Donald J. Trump

"I think I seen his bumper sticker once."   Random Idaho
truck driver

"Memento mori." (Remember, you must die.)   Socrates

Printed in Great Britain
by Amazon

16294596R00082